THE BEST PET NAME BOOK EVER

Wayne Bryant Eldridge, DVM

Illustrations by Tom Kerr

New York • London • Toronto • Sydney

Excerpts from *Old Possum's Book of Practical Cats* by T.S. Eliot, copyright 1939 by T. S. Eliot and renewed 1967 by Esme Valerie Eliot, reprinted by permission of Harcourt Brace Jovanovich, Inc. and Faber and Faber Limited.

Excerpts from "How to Name a Dog" copyright © 1948 James Thurber. Copyright © 1975 Helen Thurber and Rosemary A. Thurber. From *The Beast in Me and Other Animals,* published by Harcourt Brace Jovanovich, Inc.

Excerpts adapted from *The Animals' Who's Who* by Ruthven Tremain. Reprinted with permission of Charles Scribner's Sons, an imprint of Macmillan Publishing Company, and Routledge & Kegan Paul Limited. Copyright © 1982 by Ruthven Tremain.

Peanuts cartoon by Charles Schultz, copyright United Features Syndicate. Reprinted with permission of U.S.F. Inc.

Excerpt from *The Will Rogers Book* by Paula Love, copyright 1972 by Texian Publishing Company. Reprinted with permission .

About the Author
Wayne Bryant Eldridge is a veterinarian, as well as founder and past president of Eldridge Animal Hospital and Pets First Veterinary Centers in San Antonio, Texas. He has written many articles for the general public on veterinary medicine. He is married and has three children.

All inquiries should be addressed to:
Barron's Educational Series, Inc.
250 Wireless Boulevard
Hauppauge, New York 11788

Library of Congress Catalog Card No. 89-18078

International Standard Book No. 0-8120-4258-1

Library of Congress Cataloging-in-Publication Data

Eldridge, Wayne.
   The Best Pet Name Book Ever / Wayne Eldridge.
      p. cm.
   ISBN 0-8120-4258-1
   1. Pets—Names. I. Title.
SF411.3E43   1989
929.9'7—dc20   89-18078
                                     CIP

PRINTED IN THE UNITED STATES OF AMERICA
0123   800   9876543

DEDICATION

This book is dedicated to my wife, Nancy, who has given me continuous support during our marriage. She has been a source of encouragement to me both in the practice of veterinary medicine and in helping me attain my goals.

ACKNOWLEDGMENTS

My parents, Adelene and Jack Eldridge, are to be commended for their unconditional love, for their guidance throughout the years, and for providing me with the means for my education.

I am very grateful to my children, Lori Marie Eldridge and Wayne Bryant Eldridge, Jr. for their faith in me and for their assistance with this book.

Thanks to Arianne Eubank Sweeney for untold hours of research and for entering the information into the computer.

Don Reis and the staff at Barron's have worked diligently and competently to make this book a reality.

I would also like to express my gratitude to Peggy Mahan of the Oakwell Library for her help in finding the many sources of reference material that were used.

CONTENTS

And out of the ground the Lord God
formed every beast of the field,
and every fowl of the air;
and brought them unto Adam
to see what he would call them: and
whatsoever Adam called every living creature,
that was the name thereof.

And Adam gave names to all cattle,
and to the fowl of the air,
and to every beast of the fields.

GENESIS 2: *19–20*

INTRODUCTION

During my eighteen years as a practicing veterinarian, the majority of recently acquired dogs and cats brought to me for their first examinations have had no names, not because of apathy on the owner's part but because of the lack of a guide in the name selection process; thus, the owners of these pets usually ask for my suggestions. The thousands of requests that I have received originally prompted me to collect unusual pet names; later, I categorized my growing list of names according to general subject areas, such as historical names and names of foods. This method of categorization has helped hundreds of my clients choose names–not just any name, but a unique one–for their pets. Consequently, I have decided to organize my categories into a book so that I can assist a wider range of pet owners.

The Best Pet Name Book Ever is a creative guide for naming those special animals in our lives. Some of the names in this book are the actual names of my patients taken from the files of my animal hospital; others come from interviews with pet owners, and the remainder results from research into the various categories into which I have classified the names. This book seeks to give you an overview of examples of pet names (in particular, those for dogs and cats, but not exclusively), and by no means constitutes a complete list, for the possibilities are limitless. You should use *The Best Pet Name Book Ever*, then, not as the comprehensive source on this subject, but rather as a tool to spark your imagination.

When choosing one of the names from this book or one of your own invention, you should keep in mind a couple of helpful hints. First, pick a name that your pet can easily recognize. Cats and dogs respond better to one and two syllable words: "Ezekiel" is a creative choice; however, your cat will respond more readily to the shortened "Ziggy" or "Zeke" Also, avoid giving your dog a name that sounds like one of the basic commands ("No," "Down," "Sit," "Stay," "Come," etc.). A dog named "Star" may have difficulty distinguishing her name from "Stay." Nevertheless, do not let these considerations restrict your creativity. If you are determined to name your cat "Dante Alighieri," do so, but plan on calling him "Dan" or "Ali." You can still tell your friends about the famous person for whom the cat is named.

Note: If another name within the same chapter appears in the body of an entry, SMALL CAPITALS make reference to that name–for example:

Cyprus   The island where APHRODITE was born.

"Pretty Boy"

CHAPTER 1

Appearance

What's in a name? That which we call a rose
By any other name would smell as sweet.

William Shakespeare
from *Romeo and Juliet*

The most obvious and simplest way to name a pet is by its appearance. This basis for choosing a name works especially well for a new pet whose personality and peculiarities have not yet revealed themselves to you; however, you must keep in mind that as a pet ages, its appearance may change and the name you originally chose for your animal may no longer apply. For example, "Fur Ball" is a cute name for a kitten but may not suit a fully grown tomcat. Still, such a situation rarely occurs, and basing your pet's name on its appearance can result in a fascinating and appropriate name.

Agate	Blackberry	Cali	Curly
Amber	Blackie	Calico	Curry
Angus Bull	Blacky	Calley	Daffy
Ashes	Blanca	Carbon	Dinky
Baby Bear	Blanco	Carmel	Dog
Baby Boy	Blanquita	Caspar	Doll
Baby Doll	Blondie	Charcoal	Domino
Baby Girl	Blue	Charmin	Droopy
Baby Kitty	Bob Cat	Checkers	Dusty
Badger	Boots	Chiquita	Ebony
Bandit	Bootsie	Chocolate	Eight Ball
Bat Cat	Boxcar	Cinder	Elkie
Bear	Brandy	Cinnamon	Fancy
Big Boy	Brown Spots	Clay	Fang
Big Foot	Brownie	Coco	Fat Cat
Big 'n	Browny	Coco Bear	Fawn
Big One	Buffey	Cocoa	Feather(s)
Big Red	Buffie	Cookie	Floppy
Biscuit	Buffy	Copper	Flopsy
Bits	Bunny	Cotton	Fluffy
Bitsie	Bushy	Cottontail	Four Paws
Bitsy	Butter Fingers	Crackers	Foxie
Black Ace	Button	Crimson	Foxy Lady
Black Cat	Buttons	Curlie	Freckles

Frostie	Ginger	Gray Spots	Lefty
Frosty	Ginger Snap	Hershey	Leo
Fudge	Gold Cat	Hi-Ho Silver	Licorice
Funny Face	Goldie	Hobbles	Little
Fuzz Ball	Gray	Honey	Little One
Fuzzy	Gray Cat	Husky	Lobo
Ghost	Gray Bear	Jumbo	Locket

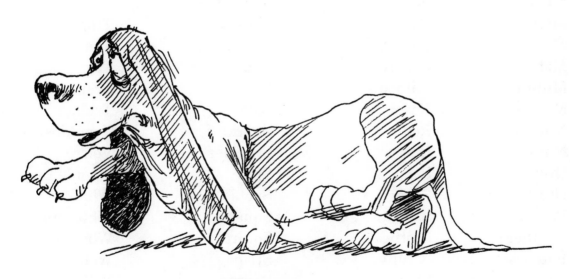

"Floppy"

Appearance

Mama Cat	Pee Wee	Shorty	Stripes
Mama Kitty	Pepper	Silky	Stripie
Manx	Perky	Slim	Tabby
Many Paws	Pig	Smidgen	Tar Baby
Midget	Piglet	Smokey	Target
Midnight	Pretty Boy	Smudge	Tawny
Minnie Paws	Pretty Girl	Sneakers	Tiger
Mitten(s)	Puff	Snow	Tiny
Momma Cat	Puffy	Snow Bear	Tip
Momma Dog	Pug	Snowball	Tippy
Moose	Pumpkin	Snowflake	Tomcat
Mother Cat	Pygmy	Snowshoes	Toy
Muffin	Rainbow	Snowy	Tramp
Munchkin	Raven	Socks	Trinket
Nugget	Red	Sparkles	Twinkles
Nutmeg	Rusty	Speckles	Velcro
Oreo	Sable	Spot	Weenie Dog
Oso	Sage	Spots	Whale
Panda	Sandy	Squat	Whiskers
Panther	Scottie	Squirt	Whitey
Patches	Scruffy	Stripe	Wolf
Paws	Shinola	Striper	Yellow

"*I think it all started when they decided to call me Happy Cat.*"

CHAPTER 2
Personality

Animals are such agreeable friends—they ask no questions, they pass no criticisms.

George Eliot (Mary Ann Cross)
from *Mr. Gilfil's Love Story*

Personality, like appearance, is one of the most obvious characteristics upon which to base a pet's name, but as I mentioned in Chapter One, a new pet's personality may not fully emerge at first, and personality, like appearance, may change as a pet grows older. While it is important to remember these considerations when choosing your pet's name, a name derived from a dominant personality trait will usually prove appropriate throughout your pet's life.

Amble	Chase	Flip	Lady
Angel	Chatterbox	Friskie	Lefty
Anxious	Chewie	Frisky	Leo
Apathy	Chewy	Front Porch Cat	Licker
Attack	Comet	Fury	Licky
Audacious Lady	Cool	Ginger Snapper	Lightnin'
Baby Bear	Couch Potato	Goofy	Loner
Baby Kitty	Crash	Grumpy	Lonesome
Back Talk	Crazy	Gunner	Lover
Bad Cat	Cuddles	Gypsy	Lover Boy
Badger	Daffy	Happy	Lover Girl
Ballerina	Dandy	Happy Cat	Lovey
Bandit	Dash	Hiccup	Lucky
Banshee	Demon	Hobo	Magic
Bear	Dennis the	Hokey	Mama Trouble
Blue	Menace	Honey	Meow
Bomber	Digger	Hoover	Mew
Bonkers	Dr. Jekyll	Hot Dog	Mew-Mew
Bully	Duster	Hunter	Mischief
Candy	Fearless	Jet	Miss Piggy
Chainsaw	Finesse	Jinx	Miss Priss
Chance	Flake	Jumper	Miss Sassy
Chancy	Flakey	Killer	Moody
Charmer	Flash	Kinky	Motor

Mouser	Schitzo	Spunky	Troubles
Moxy	Scooter	Squeaky	Trusty
Mr. Hyde	Scout	Squiggles	Tuffy
Nibbler	Scrapper	Stray	Tugger
Nibbles	Scrappy	Stray Cat	Vagrant
Noble	Shadow	Taffy	Valiant
Oddball	Shock	Tiger	Wags
Peppy	Shocker	Tom	Warrior
Play Kitty	Sissy	Tough Cat	Watchcat
Pokey	Skamp	Tramp	Watchdog
Prancer	Skamper	Trip	Wiggles
Prissy	Sleepy	Tripper	Winker
Puddles	Slipper	Trooper	Winky
Radar	Slumber		
Rambler	Snapback		
Ranger	Snapper		
Rascal	Snappy		
Rebel	Sneaky		
Rover	Sniffer		
Rowdy	Sniffles		
Runner	Sniffy		
Sassy	Snuggles		
Scamp	Solo		
Scarlet	Spooky		

"Jacques" *(and friend)*

CHAPTER 3

Human Names

The Naming of Cats is a difficult matter,
. . .First of all, there's the name that the family uses daily,
Such as Victor or Jonathan, George or Bill Bailey–
All of them sensible everyday names.
There are fancier names if you think they sound sweeter,
Some for the gentlemen, some for the dames:
Such as Plato, Admetus, Electra, Demeter . . .

T.S. Eliot
from *Old Possum's Book of Practical Cats*

A pet with a human name tends to have a special relationship with its owner, who often regards the pet as a surrogate child or best friend. In fact, many owners name their pets after a person they have known, a relative, or someone they admire. Frequently, a human name can best depict the character, or nature, of a pet; for instance, "Reginald" vividly suggests the qualities of a basset hound. Likewise, a pet may resemble—hopefully not to a great extent—someone you know. If you can name your pet after this person without offending him or her, then you have further established your pet's unique identity.

Human Names

Aaron
Abby
Abe
Abigail
Adam
Adelene
Agatha
Agnes
Al
Albert
Alex
Alexander
Alfred
Alice
Alison
Allison
Amanda
Amelia
Amos
Amy
André
Andrea
Andy
Angela

Ann
Anna
Anne
Annie
April
Armstrong
Arnie
Arnold
Arthur
Ashley
Audrey
Babette
Bailey
Barbie
Barkley
Barnaby
Barney
Barnie
Barry
Bart
Bartholomew
Basil
Bea
Beau

Becky
Belle
Ben
Benji
Bentley
Bernard
Bernie
Bert
Bertha
Beth
Betsy
Bianca
Bill
Billie
Billy
Billy Bob
Blaire
Bobbi
Bobby
Bonnie
Bosley
Brad
Bradley
Brady

Brando
Brandon
Brandy
Brent
Brett
Brewster
Brian
Bridget
Bridgette
Britt
Brooke
Brooks
Bruce
Bruno
Brutus
Bryant
Bubba
Bubba Smith
Buck
Bud
Buddy
Burt
Butch
Byron

Calvin	Chester	Connie	Dexter
Cammie	Chet	Courtney	Diana
Cammy	Christina	Craig	Dodie
Candice	Christopher	Crystal	Dody
Carley	Chris	Curt	Dollie
Carmella	Chuck	Curtis	Dolly
Carmen	Ciel	Daisy	Dominic
Carol	Cindy	Dale	Don
Casey	Clancy	Damon	Donald
Casper	Clara	Dan	Donna
Cassidy	Clare	Dana	Donnie
Cassie	Clark	Danielle	Dory
Caterina	Claudia	Danny	Dot
Cathy	Clay	Daphne	Dottie
Catrina	Clem	Darcy	Doug
Cecil	Clementine	Darren	Douglas
Celia	Cleo	David	Drew
Charles	Cliff	Davy	Dudley
Charley	Clifford	Dawn	Duncan
Charlie	Clint	Debbie	Dustin
Charlotte	Clinton	Dee	Dwayne
Chaz	Colby	Dennis	Dylan
Chelsea	Colette	Derek	Earl
Cher	Colline	Derrick	Edgar

Edie	Fay	Gertrude	Herbie
Edward	Felicia	Gina	Herman
Edwin	Felix	Ginger	Hilary
Edy	Fletch	Ginnie	Hilda
Elaine	Flo	Ginny	Hollis
Eli	Floyd	Gloria	Holly
Ellie	Francine	Golda	Howard
Elliot	Frank	Grace	Huey
Elsa	Frankie	Gracey	Ian
Elsie	Frannie	Gracie	Ilsa
Elvira	Fred	Greg	Inga
Emilio	Freddie	Gretta	Ingrid
Emily	Freddy	Gunther	Irving
Emma	Frederick	Gussie	Ivan
Eric	Gabby	Gwen	Jack
Erin	Gary	Haley	Jackie
Ernest	Gayle	Harold	Jacob
Ethan	Gene	Harry	Jacques
Eunice	George	Harv	Jake
Eva	Georgette	Harvey	James
Evan	Georgia	Hattie	Jamie
Ezra	Gerard	Hazel	Jan
Faith	Gerrie	Heather	Jane
Fannie	Gertie	Henry	Janie

Jason	Jody	Katherine	Lee
Jasper	Joe	Kathy	Lena
Jean	Joel	Katie	Leroy
Jedgar	Joela	Katy	Leslie
Jeffrey	Joey	Kay	Lianna
Jen	John	Kelly	Libby
Jennie	John Alex	Kent	Lilly
Jennifer	John Henry	Kerry	Linda
Jenny	Johnny	Kevin	Lindsay
Jeremy	Jonathan	Kim	Lisa
Jerry	Joni	Kimberly	Liz
Jess	Jonie	Kimbrey	Liza
Jesse	Josh	Kit	Lois
Jessica	Joseph	Kristen	Lola
Jessie	Josephine	Kristie	Lollie
Jill	Josie	Kristy	Lora
Jim	Joya	Lacey	Lori
Jimmie	Joyce	Lacie	Lottie
Jimmy	Judy	Lance	Lou
Joan	Julie	Lanna	Louie
Joann	Julius	Laura	Luigi
Joanne	Justin	Lauren	Louis
Jock	Karen	Lea	Louise
Jodie	Kate	Leanne	Lucas

Lucy	Marvin	Miles	Nellie
Luke	Mathilda	Millie	Nelly
Maddy	Matt	Mindy	Nicholas
Madeline	Matthew	Mira	Nick
Maggie	Mattie	Miriam	Nicky
Magnum	Maureen	Missy	Nicole
Malcolm	Maven	Misty	Niki
Mandy	Mavis	Mitch	Noel
Mangus	Max	Molly	Nora
Marcey	Maxine	Montgomery	Norman
Marcia	May	Monty	Olive
Marcie	Maynard	Morris	Oliver
Marcus	McGee	Muriel	Ollie
Marge	Meagan	Murphy	Oscar
Margie	Meg	Murray	Otto
Margo	Megan	Nadine	Pam
Maria	Melissa	Nance	Pamela
Marianne	Melvin	Nancy	Parker
Mark	Mia	Naomi	Patrick
Marlene	Michael	Natalie	Patty
Marsha	Michelle	Nathan	Paula
Marshie	Mickey	Ned	Pearl
Martha	Mike	Neil	Peg
Martin	Mikey	Nell	Peggy

Penelope	Ricky	Sandy	Sophie
Percival	Riley	Sara	Stacey
Percy	Rita	Sarah	Stanley
Pete	Robert	Saul	Stephanie
Petra	Robin	Schroder	Stephen
Petula	Roger	Schultz	Stuart
Phil	Ron	Scott	Sue
Philip	Ronald	Scottie	Susan
Phoebe	Ronney	Sean	Susie
Phyllis	Ronnie	Sebastian	Susy
Polly	Roscoe	Seth	Suzanne
Priscilla	Rose	Seymour	Suzette
Prudy	Roxanne	Shannon	Suzie
Rachel	Roy	Shawn	Suzy
Ralph	Rudy	Shayne	Sylvia
Randy	Russell	Sheila	Tamara
Raquel	Rusty	Shelby	Tammy
Raymond	Ruth	Shelly	Tanya
Reba	Ryan	Sherry	Ted
Rebecca	Sabrina	Shirley	Teddy
Reginald	Sadie	Sibyl	Teena
Rex	Sally	Sid	Teresa
Rhett	Sam	Sidney	Teri
Rick	Samantha	Simon	Tessa

Human Names

Tessi	Tony	Vick	William
Tessie	Tracy	Vicky	Willie
Theodore	Travis	Victor	Willy
Thomas	Trudy	Virginia	Wilma
Tiffany	Tucker	Wally	Windy
Timmy	Tyler	Walter	Winnie
Timothy	Valerie	Warren	Winston
Tina	Van	Wayne	Woodrow
Toby	Vanessa	Webster	Zachary
Tom	Vera	Wendy	Zeke
Tommy	Vic	Wilbur	

"Honey Bunny"

CHAPTER 4

Terms of Endearment

I am driven to the conclusion that my sense of kinship with animals is greater than most people feel. It amuses me to talk to animals in a sort of jargon I have invented for them; and it seems to me that it amuses them to be talked to, and they respond to the tone of the conversation, though its intellectual content may to some extent escape them.

George Bernard Shaw
from *Killing for Sport*

Many people use terms of endearment to refer to members of their families. A large number of people also use such terms when addressing their pets. Names such as "Baby" and "Sweetie" may not have originally been a dog's or cat's name, but by repeated use, an owner may come to refer to his or her pet in that manner. Many owners, however, initially choose a term of endearment for a special pet's name, and often the owner will create this affectionate name from his or her own heart.

Terms of Endearment

Ace	Fu Fu	Kissy Bear	Puddin'
Angel	Fuffy	Kissy Face	Punkin
Babe	Gin Gin	Kitter	Sugar
Baby	Ginger Sugar	Lad	Sugar 'n Spice
Baby Bear	Gingi Girl	Laddie	Sugar Bear
Baby Doll	Girly	Lov-a-Lot	Sugarkins
Baby Girl	Hey Girl	Lover Boy	Sugar Pie
Baby Kitty	Honey	Lover Girl	Sugar Plum
Beau Beau	Honey Blue	Lovey	Sugarfoot
Bitsie	Honey Bunny	Lovey Lou	Sunshine
Bitsy	Honey Dew	Lovums	Sweet Pea
Buffer	Hot Dog	Marshmallow	Sweetie
Duster	Hotlips	Patty Cake	Sweetie Pie
Dusty	Itsy-Bitsy	Precious	Sweetums
Fifi	Junior	Pudden	True Blue
Fluffer	Keeper		

"Washington"

CHAPTER 5
Historical Names

I never have been able to get very far in the exploration of the minds of people who call their dogs Mussolini, Tojo, and Adolph, and I suspect the reason is that I am unable to associate with them long enough to examine what goes on in their heads. I nod, and I tell them the time of day, if they ask, and that is all.

James Thurber
from *"How to Name a Dog"*

Many owners choose historical names for their pets, either because they enjoy history or because a particular historical figure interests them, and sometimes, a pet may actually resemble a well-known character from history. For instance, the name "Napoleon Bonaparte" would accurately describe a small feisty dog. This chapter contains the names of some famous—and some not-so-famous—dogs and cats of the past and a sampling of the names of the prominent figures of world history. The list of the latter is by no means complete; it only illustrates some of the names that other pet owners have used.

Historical Names

Agrippina   The mother of the Roman emperor NERO. He had her murdered.

Alexander   (1) The name of three of the Russian Czars. (2) Alexander of Macedonia, conqueror of the ancient world, who was known as "Alexander the Great."

Ambrose (Saint)   A bishop of Milan in the fourth century A.D. who was one of the most influential men of his time.

Appleseed, Johnny   John Chapman (1774–1845). The orchards of the Midwest grew from the seed that this nurseryman was reported to have spread across the land.

Attila   King of the Huns called the "Scourge of God" by peoples he conquered during the fifth century.

Balto   A black, long-haired malamute that in February, 1925 led Gunnar Kasson's dog team through a blizzard to reach diphtheria-plagued Nome, Alaska with antitoxin serum. A statue of Balto stands in New York City's Central Park.

Beau   Gen. Omar BRADLEY's pet poodle.

Beauregard   A Confederate general whose full name was Pierre Gustave Toutant de Beauregard.

Bessie   A collie that belonged to President Calvin Coolidge, the thirtieth President of the United States (1923–1929).

Billy the Kid   William Bonney (1859–1881). A ruthless Wild West criminal who killed a man before reaching his teens.

Bingo   The black and white dog on Cracker Jack boxes.

Bismarck	Otto Eduard Leopold von Bismarck (1815–1898), a Prussian statesman who united the German states into one empire and created the Triple Alliance between Germany, Austria-Hungary and Italy, thus preserving peace in Europe until World War I.
Blackberry	One of President Calvin Coolidge's pet dogs.
Blackie	A mixed breed dog that belonged to the author when he was a child.
Blacky	President Calvin Coolidge's black cat.
Blanco	A white collie that a little girl in Illinois gave to President Lyndon B. Johnson during his term in office.
Bluegrass	Daniel BOONE's family cat.
Bonham	A hero of the Battle of the Alamo (1836).
Boone (Daniel)	Hero of the early West who was a famous Indian fighter and frontiersman.
Bradley (Omar Nelson)	An American general who commanded troops in Europe in World War II.
Brutus	The Roman general and orator who led the plot to murder Julius Caesar in 44 B.C.
Buddy	The female German shepherd who was the first Seeing Eye dog. Buddy belonged to Morris Frank, a blind man from Tennessee, and was trained in Switzerland at the kennels where Dorothy Harrison Eustis, the founder of The Seeing Eye Inc., worked. Frank told Buddy's story in his book, *First Lady of Seeing Eye*.

Historical Names

Buffalo Bill	William Cody (1846–1917), was a famous hunter and scout who starred in and operated his own Wild West show.
Caesar (Julius)	The Roman general and statesman who became dictator of Rome, ending the era of the Roman Republic.
Charlemagne	The great military leader who became the first Holy Roman Emperor from A.D. 800–814.
Checkers	A black-and-white cocker spaniel sent to Richard Nixon when he was running for vice president. Nixon revealed Checkers' existence when he appeared on television on September 23, 1952, to combat allegations that he had received illegal campaign funds. His speech has since been called the Checkers Speech.
Chips	A shepherd-husky-collie mix that was the first member of the army's K-9 Corps sent overseas in World War II. Chips landed in Sicily in July 1943 and aided pinned-down American troops by attacking Italian gunners. He received decorations for this act and returned home in 1945.
Cicero	The statesman and orator who tried to save the dying Roman Republic.
Cloe	A dog that belonged to George Washington, first President of the United States (1789–1797).
Crockett (Davy)	Famous frontiersman who died at the Battle of the Alamo (1836).
Cuba	One of Ernest Hemingway's forty cats.
Custer (George Armstrong)	The famous American army officer who lost his life in a battle against the Indians at Little Bighorn, which has become known as Custer's Last Stand.

Fala	The Scottish terrier that Franklin D. Roosevelt humorously defended against unjustified attacks by his political opponents.
Ferdinand	A king of Spain who, with his wife Isabella, received Christopher Columbus at the Court in Barcelona and agreed to finance his voyage.
Fido	The yellow mongrel belonging to Abraham Lincoln's two sons, Willie and Tad. Fido stayed behind in Springfield, Illinois when the President-elect and his family moved to Washington.
Gandhi (Mohandas Karamchand)	The great Indian statesman (1869–1948) who freed his country from British rule through nonviolent resistance. Gandhi is considered the father of modern India.
Genghis Khan	The great Mongol ruler (1167–1227) who conquered a vast empire, including China.
Golda Meir	The woman who became Prime Minister of Israel in 1969.
Handsome Dan	The white bulldog that was the original Yale bulldog mascot. The first Handsome Dan has been followed by a series of namesakes, one of which still represents Yale today.
Her	One of the pair of beagles that accompanied President Lyndon B. Johnson and his family to the White House. Johnson received much criticism when he lifted Her and the other beagle HIM up by the ears.
Him	The other half of President Lyndon B. Johnson's pair of beagles. (See HER)
Hitler (Adolph)	The totalitarian ruler of Germany's Third Reich who initiated World War II and was responsible for the slaughter of millions of people.

Historical Names

Houdini (Harry) The famous magician (1874–1926) who could escape from any contraption devised to hold him.

Igloo The troublesome fox terrier that traveled with Adm. Richard E. Byrd on his first trip to the Antarctic (1928–1930).

Ike The nickname of Dwight David Eisenhower, the Supreme Commander of the Allied armies in Europe in World War II. Eisenhower later became President of the United States (1953–1961).

Isabella Queen of Spain and wife of FERDINAND.

Ivan The name of several Russian rulers. Ivan IV (1533–1584), known as "Ivan the Terrible," was the first Russian czar.

James (Jesse) The notorious bank and train robber who vandalized the American West during the nineteenth century.

Jo-Fi Psychoanalyst Sigmund Freud's beloved chow.

Lady One of George Washington's pet dogs.

Laika The female Samoyed that was the first living creature to orbit the earth in the second Soviet Sputnik.

Livingstone (David) A famous British explorer who pioneered large parts of Africa during the nineteenth century.

Magellan (Ferdinand) The Portugese navigator who was the first person to sail around the world.

Major	A German shepherd that belonged to Franklin Delano Roosevelt.
Marco	A Pomeranian that belonged to Queen Victoria of England.
Marco Polo	A Venetian who was one of the first Europeans to travel in Asia during the late thirteenth century.
Marjorie	A diabetic black-and-white mongrel that was the first creature to be kept alive by insulin.
Maximilian	The Austrian whom the French installed as emperor of the short-lived Mexican throne (1864–1867).
Meggy	One of Franklin D. Roosevelt's pet dogs. FALLA was Meggy's sire.
Micetto	Pope Leo XII's large black-striped cat. After the Pope's death, the cat went to live with the French ambassador to Rome, the Vicomte de Chateaubriand.
Ming	The dynasty that ruled China from 1368 to 1644. The Ming period was one of artistic growth.
Montgomery (Bernard Law)	The British general who won fame during the African campaign and the invasion of Europe in World War II.
Mopsey	One of George Washington's favorite dogs.
Mushka	A dog that was placed in orbit by the Russians in one of the first Sputnik space vehicles.

Historical Names

Napoleon (Bonaparte)	The French general and military genius (1769–1821) who crowned himself Emperor of France and conquered much of Europe.
Neff (Pat)	A governor of Texas during the first half of the twentieth century and a president of Baylor University in Waco, Texas.
Nelson	A black cat, the favorite of Sir Winston Churchill, Prime Minister of Great Britain during most of World War II.
Nelson (Horatio)	Great Britain's greatest admiral and naval hero, who established Britain's rule of the seas in the 1800's.
Nero	One of the cruelest Roman emperors, who killed thousands of Christians.
Newton (Sir Isaac)	The English scientist, astronomer, and mathematician (1642–1727) who invented calculus and first established the laws of gravity.
Niña, Pinta, and Santa Maria	The three ships in Christopher Columbus's fleet when he discovered America on October 12, 1492.
Nipper	The fox terrier that appears with a phonograph in the RCA trademark.
Patton (George Smith)	An American general (1885–1945) who led the 3rd Army in Europe during World War II.
Pavlov (Ivan Petrovich)	The Russian physiologist who won the 1904 Nobel Prize in physiology and medicine for his research on conditioned reflexes.
Perruque	One of 14 cats owned by Cardinal Richelieu, when he died in 1642.
Pushinka	A puppy from STRELKA's litter which the Soviet Premier Nikita Khrushchev presented to Mrs. John F. Kennedy when she was First Lady.

Reagan (Ronald)	The motion picture actor and California governor who became the fortieth President of the United States.
Ripley (Robert Leroy)	An American cartoonist who began collecting strange and unusual facts which he eventually compiled into two *Believe It or Not* books.
Rommel (Erwin)	The brilliant German general (1891–1944) who commanded the Afrika Korps and the forces defending Normandy in World War II.
Ross (Betsy)	Creator of the first U.S. flag.
Sailor Boy	Theodore Roosevelt's pet dog.
Scannon	Meriwether Lewis's black Newfoundland that accompanied the Lewis and Clark expedition to the Pacific.
Searcher	One of Geroge Washington's pet dogs.
Shannon	A dog that was the White House pet of of John F. Kennedy, Jr.
Shasta	The first United States-born *liger*, the offspring of a male lion and a female tiger, to reach maturity. Shasta was born May 6, 1948, at the Hogle Zoological Garden in Salt Lake City, Utah.
Sizi	The cat that was a companion to Albert Schweitzer (1875–1965) when he was a medical missionary in Africa.
Stanley (Henry)	The British explorer who led the expedition to find David LIVINGSTON.
Strelka	One of the two female Samoyed that the Soviet Union launched in Sputnik V on August 19, 1960.
Thatcher (Margaret)	The Prime Minister of Great Britain who is known as the "Iron Lady."

Historical Names

Tito *A Jackson brother* The Communist ruler of Yugoslavia after World War II. Tito declared Yugoslavia's independence from Soviet control.

Trafalgar The cape on Spain's southern coast at the western entrance to the Strait of Gibraltar which was the sight of one of history's greatest naval battles: Great Britain, led by Admiral Horatio Nelson, defeated the combined French and Spanish fleets on October 21, 1805.

Trojan *Condom* An inhabitant of Troy, an ancient city in Asia Minor that Homer made famous.

Uncle Sam The personification of the United States; his top hat and red, white, and blue clothes make him a distinctive figure.

Viking A member of the Scandinavian bands of sea rovers who raided England, Ireland, France, Germany, Italy, and Spain between the 700s and 1100s. The Vikings also settled Greenland and Iceland.

Washington (George) Commander of the American forces during the Revolutionary War and first President of the United States

Winston (Churchill) The Prime Minister of Great Britain from 1940 to 1945 and from 1951 to 1955, who was one of world history's greatest statesmen.

Wright (Orville and Wilbur) Credited with flying the first airplane at Kitty Hawk, North Carolina, December 17, 1903.

Yuki The small white dog adopted by President Lyndon B. Johnson in November 1966. Yuki quickly became the President's favorite dog.

"Winston"

ATHENA

CHAPTER 6

Greek and Roman Mythology

Far from Italy, far from my native Tarentum I lie;
And this is the worst of it—worse than death.
An exile's life is no life. But the Muses loved me.
For my suffering they gave me a honeyed gift:
My name survives me. Thanks to the Sweet Muses.
Leonidas will echo through all time.

Leonidas of Tarentum
from *The Greek Anthology*

The gods, goddesses, and other figures of mythology are known for both their colorful appearance and their vibrant personalities; furthermore, they generally have unusual, and therefore, memorable names. Thus, pets often are namesakes of these characters, and a pet's mythological name can provide a great source of conversation.

Achelous	A river god who turned himself into a bull to fight Heracles (see HERCULES) because the two men were both in love with the same woman, Deianira.
Achilles	The champion of the Greeks in the Trojan War.
Actaeon	A young hunter whom ARTEMIS turned into a stag because he had accidentally seen her naked. In his new form, ACTAEON's own dogs chased and killed him.
Adonis	APHRODITE's love, who spent half the year with her and the other half in the Underworld. A boar killed him, and a crimson flower sprung up where each drop of his blood fell.
Aeneas	The son of APHRODITE (Venus) who fought for Troy in the Trojan War. After the defeat he escaped to Italy where he founded the Roman race.
Aero	ORION's love and the daughter of the King of Chios.
Aidos	The personified emotion of reverence and shame, which was esteemed highest of all feelings.
Ajax	One of the Greek champions in the Trojan War.
Alce	One of ACTAEON's hounds; the name means "strength."
Alexander	Another name for PARIS, who caused the Trojan War and died of a wound from a poisoned arrow.
Althea	The mother of Meleager; she killed him and then killed herself.
Amarynthos	One of ACTAEON's hounds.

Amazon	A member of the nation of women warriors who had no dealings with men except to oppose them in war and to breed children.
Andromache	The devoted wife of HECTOR, prince of TROY.
Andromeda	The daughter of CASSIOPEIA, who was punished for her mother's vanity. PERSEUS saved her from her fate, and she married him.
Antigone	The daughter of OEDIPUS. She was killed by CREON, his successor on the throne.
Aphrodite	The Goddess of Love and Beauty.
Apollo	The God of Light and Truth.
Arcas	The son of CALLISTO and ZEUS whom Zeus placed among the stars as Ursa Minor (Lesser Bear).
Ares	The God of War (Roman: Mars). The Son of ZEUS and HERA; he was a bully and also a coward, detested by his parents as well as others.
Argonauts	JASON and his followers who went on a quest to bring back the GOLDEN FLEECE. Their ship was the Argo.
Argos	ODYSSEUS's dog. After being away at the Trojan War for twenty years, Odysseus returned to his home disguised as a beggar, and only Argos recognized him. The dog, too sick and weak to walk, wagged his tail in recognition; however, afraid of revealing his identity, Odysseus didn't acknowledge Argos, and as Odysseus walked on, Argos died.
Argus	HERA's watchman with a hundred eyes.

Ariadne	King MINOS's daughter who was deserted on the island of NAXOS by her lover, THESEUS.
Arion	The first horse, an offspring of POSEIDON.
Arne	Regarded as the ancestress of the Boeotian Greeks.
Artemis	The Goddess of Hunting and Wild Things.
Asbolos	One of ACTAEON's hounds; the name means "soot-color."
Asopus	A river god.
Astraea	The daughter of ZEUS and THEMIS. She lived on earth happily during the Golden Age, but fled during the Bronze Age.
Atalanta	The maiden who could outshoot, outrun, and outwrestle most men. She eventually was turned into a lioness.
Ate	The Goddess of Mischief. Although a daughter of ZEUS, she was cast out of OLYMPUS.
Athena	The Goddess of the City, Protector of Civilized Life, Handicrafts, and Agriculture.
Atlas	The TITAN who held the world on his shoulders.
Attica	The country around Athens.
Aurora	The Goddess of Dawn.
Bacchus	Roman name for DIONYSUS, the God of the Vine.

Banos One of ACTAEON's hounds.

Battus A peasant who saw HERMES steal APOLLO's cattle. Hermes turned Battus into stone because the man broke his promise not to reveal the identity of the thief to Apollo.

Baucis A poor old woman was blessed by the gods, given a temple to live in, and promised that she would never live alone without her husband.

Bellona The Roman name for ENYO, the Goddess of War.

Belus The grandfather of the Danaïds (who were condemned to carry water in jars that were forever leaking.)

Biton One of the two sons of Cydippe, a priestess of HERA. He and his brother yoked themselves to a wagon to carry their mother to pray. The journey killed both sons.

Boötes The constellation just behind the Dipper. See ICARIUS.

Boreas (1) The God of the North Wind who kidnapped and ravished Orithyia. (2) One of ACTAEON's hounds.

Bromius Another name for DIONYSUS, who was a son of ZEUS. (See BACCHUS.)

Brontes One of three CYCLOPS, each of whom had only one eye in the middle of his forehead.

Cabeiri Dwarfs with supernatural powers. They protected the fields of Lemnos.

Cacus The giant who stole cattle from Heracles (HERCULES) flock.

Calliope	The daughter of ZEUS who was the MUSE of Epic Poetry.
Callisto	LYCAON's daughter who was seduced by ZEUS and bore him a son, ARCAS. In a jealous rage, HERA turned Callisto into a bear, and when Arcas grew up placed his mother before him so that he would kill her. Zeus, however, saved Callisto and put her up in the stars as Ursa Major (Great Bear), placing Arcas beside her as Ursa Minor (Lesser Bear).
Calpe	The ancient Greek name for the Rock of Gibraltar.
Calypso	A nymph who kept ODYSSEUS prisoner on her island.
Camilla	A very skilled maiden warrior who was followed by a band of warriors.
Canache	One of ACTAEON's hounds; the name means "ringwood."
Cassandra	One of PRIAM's daughters. She became a prophetess because APOLLO loved her and gave her power of prognostication. Unfortunately, her prophecies were never believed.
Cassiopeia	ANDROMEDA's mother, the Ethiopian queen, who was silly and vain and bragged that Andromeda was prettier than the daughters of the sea god NEREUS.
Castor	The brother of POLLUX and the son of LEDA. He and his brother were the Protectors of Sailors.
Centaur	A creature who was half man and half horse.
Cerberus	The huge, fearsome watchdog of HADES. Cerberus guarded the gates of Hades, preventing spirits from leaving.

Ceres | The Roman name for DEMETER.

Chaos | The Nothingness that existed before the gods and before Creation.

Charites | Another name for the Graces who attended APHRODITE.

Charon | The boatman who guided the ferry that carried the dead souls to the gates of HADES.

Chediatros | One of ACTAEON's hounds.

Circe | A beautiful and dangerous witch who turned men into beasts.

Cisseta | One of ACTAEON's hounds.

Cleobis | BITON's brother, son of Cydippe, a priestess of HERA. Cleobis perished with his brother after they yoked themselves to a wagon carrying their mother to pray.

Clio | The MUSE of History.

Clytie | A maiden who loved the Sun God, but whose love was not returned. She stared at him with longing until she turned into a sunflower.

Cora | Another name for PERSEPHONE.

Coran | One of ACTAEON's hounds; the name means "crop-eared."

Cornucopia | The Horn of Plenty. Named after the horn of the goat, it was always full of food and drink.

Coronis	A maiden whom APOLLO loved, but who did not love him. She was unfaithful, so he killed her.
Cottus	A monster with a hundred hands.
Creon	The brother of JOCASTA. Creon became regent after OEDIPUS resigned the throne.
Cronus	A TITAN who was the father of ZEUS.
Cupid	Latin for EROS, the Greek God of Love.
Cyclops	A giant with only one eye in the middle of his forehead.
Cyllo	One of ACTAEON's hounds; the name means "halt."
Cyllopotes	One of ACTAEON's hounds; the name means "zigzagger."
Cynthia	Another name for ARTEMIS.
Cyprian	Another name for APHRODITE.
Cyprios	One of ACTAEON's hounds.
Cyprus	The island where APHRODITE was born.
Dactyls	The women of Mount Ida, who were the first to make implements of iron.
Daphne	A huntress whose father, the river god Peneus, changed her into a tree to protect her from APOLLO who loved her.
Delian	Another name for APOLLO.

Delos — The island where APOLLO was born and where his temple stood.

Delphi — The site of APOLLO's oracles.

Demeter — The Goddess of Corn. Sister of ZEUS, she bore him a daughter, PERSEPHONE.

Diana — The Roman name for ARTEMIS.

Dido — The founder and queen of Carthage. She threw herself on a pyre when AENEAS, whom she loved, left to search for a homeland in Italy.

Diomedes — A great Greek warrior at TROY.

Dione — A minor goddess. By some accounts, Dione and Zeus were APHRODITE's parents.

Dionysus — The God of the Vine.

Dirce — The wife of LYCUS, the ruler of THEBES. Her grandsons and daughter killed her by tying her hair to a bull.

Dodona — ZEUS's oracle, the oldest in Greece.

Dorian — A member of one of the prinicpal groups of ancient Greeks.

Doris — One of the three-thousand daughters of Ocean and wife NEREUS.

Draco — One of ACTAEON's hounds; the name means "the dragon."

Dromas — One of ACTAEON's hounds; the name means "the courser."

Dromios — One of ACTAEON's hounds; the name means "seize 'em."

Dryad	One of the nymphs of the trees.
Echnobas	One of ACTAEON's hounds.
Echo	The fairest of the nymphs who loved NARCISSUS; HERA condemned her never to talk unless she repeated what someone else had already said.
Electra	The daughter of Agamemnon and Clytemnestra. She avenged her father's murder by inciting her brother, Orestes, to kill their mother and her lover.
Enyo	The Goddess of War.
Ephialtes	A giant. He and his twin brother wanted to prove themselves superior to the gods. For their presumption ARTEMIS killed them by making them accidentally slay each other.
Erato	The MUSE of Love Poetry.
Erigone	The daughter of ICARIUS, who hanged herself after finding her father murdered. DIONYSUS placed her in the heavens as Virgo.
Eris	The sister of ARES whose name means "Discord."
Eros	The God of Love.
Eudromos	One of ACTAEON's hounds; the name means "good runner."
Europa	A maiden with whom ZEUS fell in love. As a bull, he carried her off to Crete. The continent of Europe was named for her.

Eurus	The God of the East Wind.
Eurydice	The bride of ORPHEUS. She was killed by a viper sting after the wedding.
Fauna	The Roman Goddess of Fertility, sometimes called the Good Goddess.
Favonius	The Latin name for the West Wind.
Flora	The Roman Flower Goddess.
Galatea	(1) A sea nymph whom Polyphemus, the CYCLOPS, loved. (2) The name of PYGMALION's statue, which came to life.
Gemini	The constellation of the twin brothers, CASTOR and POLLUX.
Golden Fleece	The fleece of a ram that rescued PHRIXUS. He sacrificed it to ZEUS in thanksgiving. JASON subsequently led the quest for the Golden Fleece.
Gorgon	Dragonlike creatures with wings and snakes for hair, whose look turned men to stone.
Griffins	ZEUS's hounds, which had the bodies of lions and the heads and wings of eagles. These beasts guarded the Gold of the North.
Hades	The God of the Underworld. He was the son of CRONUS and RHEA. (Hades is also used as a name for the Underworld itself.)
Harmonia	Cadmus's wife, who was the daughter of ARES and APHRODITE.
Harpale	One of ACTAEON's hounds; the name means "voracious."

Harpeia	One of ACTAEON's hounds; the name means "tear 'em."
Harpies	Flying creatures with hooked beaks and claws, which left behind them a terrible stench that sickened all living creatures.
Hebe	The Goddess of Youth. She was the daughter of ZEUS and HERA.
Hecate	A triple deity who was Goddess of the Moon, Goddess of the Earth, and Goddess of the Underworld.
Hector	The brave, noble son of King PRIAM of TROY. Hector was the Trojan champion in the Trojan War.
Hecuba	The queen of TROY and wife of King PRIAM.
Helen	The daughter of ZEUS and LEDA, who was the fairest woman in the world. She married MENELAUS, but PARIS kidnapped her, starting the Trojan War.
Helicon	One of the MUSES' mountains. It was sacred to APOLLO whose temple was there.
Helios	The sun god.
Hephaestus	The God of Fire.
Hera	ZEUS's wife and sister. She was the Protector of Marriage and Married Women.
Heracles	See HERCULES.
Hercules	The Roman name for Heracles, Greece's greatest hero and the strongest man alive.

Hermes	ZEUS's messenger. He was sometimes called the "Master Thief."
Hermione	Unaware she had been promised to Orestes, MENELAUS gave her to ACHILLES' son, Pyrrhus.
Hero	The ill-fated lover of LEANDER. He died, and she killed herself.
Herse	An Athenian princess who was beloved by Hermes.
Hesper	The Goddess of the Evening Star.
Hesperides	The daughter of ATLAS, who with LADON (2), guarded the trees with golden branches, golden leaves, and golden apples.
Hestia	The Goddess of the Hearth.
Hilara	The daughter of APOLLO. Her name means "laughter-loving."
Himeros	The God of Desire who attended EROS. Also called Longing.
Hippodamia	Wife of PELOPS. He won her in a chariot race.
Hippolytus	The son of THESEUS whose second wife, PHAEDRA, fell in love with Hippolytus.
Hyacinth	A companion of APOLLO. He was accidentally killed when Apollo's discus hit him in the head. On each spot where a drop of his blood fell, a Hyacinth flower arose.
Hyades	Some nymphs whom ZEUS placed as the stars that bring rain when they are near the horizon.
Hydra	A nine-headed creature killed by Heracles. (See HERCULES.)

Hypnos	The God of Sleep.
Iacchus	Another name for DIONYSUS. (See BACCHUS.)
Ibycus	A poet who lived around 550 B.C. When robbers left him mortally wounded he asked the cranes that were flying overhead to avenge him, and they did.
Icarus	The son of Daedalus, the architect. When Icarus flew too near the sun, the wax that held his wings in place melted. Icarus fell to earth and was killed.
Icarius	An Athenian, in Greek mythology, whom DIONYSUS taught how to make wine. Drunken shepherds murdered Icarius and threw him down a well, where his faithful dog, MAERA, found him. Dionysus honored Icarius, placing him among the stars as the constellation BOÖTES.
Icelus	The son of HYPNOS, who had the power to change himself into all sorts of birds and animals.
Ichnobate	One of ACTAEON's hounds; the name means "tracker."
Ida	A nymph who took care of ZEUS when he was being hidden from Cronus.
Inachus	The father of IO.
Ino	The sea goddess who saved ODYSSEUS from drowning.
Io	The maiden who had an affair with ZEUS. He turned her into a white heifer to protect her from HERA's jealous wrath. Unfortunately, Io, wound up in Hera's possession and spent years trying to escape and return to her original form. Finally, Zeus restored Io's humanity, and she spent the rest of her days happily.

Iphicles	Heracles' (HERCULES) half brother.
Iris	The Goddess of the Rainbow.
Ixion	The first muderer. Ixion also attempted to seduce HERA. ZEUS sentenced him to eternal punishment in HADES, where he was tied to a wheel and lashed with serpents.
Janus	A NUMINA who became personified. Janus was the God of Good Beginnings.
Jason	The leader of the quest for the GOLDEN FLEECE.
Jocasta	OEDIPUS's mother and wife.
Jove	Another name for ZEUS.
Juna	The Roman name for HERA.
Jupiter	The Roman name for ZEUS.
Juturna	The Roman Goddess of Springs.
Kora	Another name for PERSEPHONE.
Labros	One of ACTAEON's hounds; the name means "furious."
Lacena	One of ACTAEON's hounds; the name means "lioness."
Lachne	One of ACTAEON's hounds; the name means "glossy."
Lacon	One of ACTAEON's hounds.

Ladon	(1) One of ACTAEON's hounds. (2) The serpent who guarded the Golden Apples of the HESPERIDES.
Laertes	ODYSSEUS's father.
Laius	The father of OEDIPUS. Oedipus unwittingly murdered him.
Lampos	One of ACTAEON's hounds; the name means "shining one."
Lar	A NUMINA, who was the spirit of an ancestor. Every Roman family had a Lar.
Larvae	The spirits of HADES's wicked dead, who were greatly feared.
Latinus	The great-grandson of SATURN and the king of the city of LATIUM.
Latium	A city in Italy that was conquered by AENEAS.
Latona	Another name for LETO.
Lavinia	The daughter of LATINUS and the wife of AENEAS. Together, husband and wife founded the Roman race.
Leander	HERO's lover who killed herself after he drowned swimming to a rendezvous with her.
Leda	The wife of King Tyndareus of Sparta. ZEUS, in the form of a swan, seduced her.
Lelaps	(1) One of ACTAEON's hounds; the name means "hurricane." (2) The hound destined to chase a fox until ZEUS finally changed them both to stone.
Lemures	Another name for LARVAE.

Lethe	The River of Forgetfulness in the Underworld.
Leto	Daughter of TITANS, APOLLO and ARTEMIS were her children by Zeus.
Leucos	One of ACTAEON's hounds; the name means "gray."
Liber	Another name for BACCHUS. (See DIONYSUS.)
Libera	A Roman name for PERSEPHONE. She was abducted by PLUTO, who wanted her to be queen of the Underworld.
Libitina	The Roman Goddess of the Dead.
Linus	The son of APOLLO and Psamathe. When his mother deserted him, dogs tore him apart.
Lityerses	A farmer who made strangers at his house reap. If they did less than he did, he cut off their heads, put their bodies in a sheaf, and sang a song. Heracles (HERCULES) killed him.
Lotis	A nymph who was changed into a lotus tree.
Lucina	Sometimes regarded as the Roman Goddess of Childbirth.
Luna	Latin for the Goddess of the Moon. The name Luna referred to DIANA.
Lyaeus	Another name for BACCHUS. (See DIONYSUS.)
Lycaon	A king of ATTICA and the father of CALLISTO. When he served human flesh at a banquet, ZEUS turned him into a wolf.
Lycisca	One of ACTAEON's hounds.

Lycus	Ruler of THEBES and the husband of DIRCE. His daughter killed him because of his cruelty.
Lyncea	One of ACTAEON's hounds.
Machaon	The Greeks' physician during the Trojan War.
Machimos	One of ACTAEON's hounds; the name means "boxer."
Maeander	River in Phrygia that frequently changes its course.
Maera	A faithful dog, whose master ICARIUS was murdered and thrown into a well. Maera led Icarius's daughter ERIGONE to the body. She hanged herself and the dog then jumped into the well.
Maia	VULCAN's wife. (See HEPHAETUS.)
Manes	The spirits of the good dead in HADES.
Marpessa	A maiden who chose the mortal Idas over APOLLO.
Mars	Roman name for ARES.
Medea	The daughter of King Colchias. A sorceress, she fell in love with JASON and helped him on his quest for the GOLDEN FLEECE.
Medusa	One of the GORGONS. Perseus cut off her head.
Megara	The wife of Heracles (HERCULES) and mother of three of his sons. Hercules went mad and killed them all.
Melampus	A great soothsayer whose pet snakes taught him animal language.

Melanchete	One of ACTAEON's hounds; the name means "black-coated."
Melanea	One of ACTAEON's hounds; the name means "black."
Melanion	The runner who beat ATALANTA and won her love.
Melicertes	The son of INO. After Ino and Melicertes jumped into the sea, to escape Athamas's wrath, Melicertes became a sea god.
Melpomene	The MUSE of Tragedy.
Menelaus	The brother of Agamemnon and husband of HELEN.
Menelea	One of ACTAEON's hounds.
Mentor	ODYSSEUS's most trusted friend. ATHENA disguised herself as Mentor when she appeared to TELEMACHUS.
Mercury	The Roman name for HERMES.
Metis	ZEUS's first wife, also called Prudence. Zeus swallowed her and developed a monumental headache, which eased only after ATHENA sprang from his head.
Midas	A king of Phrygia whose wish that everything he touched would turn to gold was granted.
Minerva	The Roman name for ATHENA.
Minos	One of the three judges in the Underworld.
Minotaur	A monster that was half bull and half human.

Minyas	The king of THESSALY. The ARGONAUTS sometimes called the Minyae, were his descendants.
Moira	Fate, a mysterious power stronger than the gods. One who scorned Moira would meet NEMESIS.
Molossos	One of ACTAEON's hounds.
Moly	An herb with white blossoms that HERMES gave ODYSSEUS to protect him from CIRCE's spells.
Mopsus	Soothsayer of the ARGONAUTS, he also went on the Calydonian boar hunt.
Morpheus	The God of Sleep; also called the God of Dreams.
Mors	The God of Death; also called Thanatos.
Muse	One of nine daughters of ZEUS and Mnemosyne. They were goddesses of memory and then of the arts and sciences.
Myrmidon	One of a group of soldiers who fought against the TROJANS.
Napa	One of ACTAEON's hounds; the name means "sired by a wolf."
Narcissus	A beautiful boy who scorned love despite many admiring ladies. Finally, he was cursed, fell in love with himself, and pined away for his own reflection in a pond.
Naxos	The island where THESEUS left ARIADNE.
Nebrophonos	One of ACTAEON's hounds; the name means "fawn-killer."
Neleus	One of the twin sons of TYRO and POSEIDON.

Nemean Lion, The	The ferocious lion that ravaged the valley of Nemea, until Heracles (HERCULES) strangled the beast to death.
Nemesis	The Goddess of Righteous Anger, the personified emotion esteemed highest of all feelings.
Neptune	The Roman name for POSEIDON.
Nereid	A nymph of the sea and the daughter of NEREUS.
Nereus	The Old Man of the Sea. He had the power of prophecy and could assume any form he desired.
Nessus	A centaur who gave Heracles' (HERCULES') wife, Deianira, his blood as a love potion when he was dying.
Nestor	The wisest and oldest of the Greek chieftans.
Nike	The Greek Goddess of Victory.
Notus	The God of the South Wind.
Numina	The powers that were the Roman gods before the Romans adopted the Greek ones.
Ocydroma	One of ACTAEON's hounds; the name means "swift runner."
Ocyrrhoe	A prophetess.
Odysseus	The Greek hero, of the Trojan War, known for his cunning.
Oedipus	The king who was fated to kill his father and marry his mother.

Olympus	A mountain peak in Greece and home of the gods.
Ophion	A great serpent that ruled the TITANS before CRONUS.
Ops	The wife of SATURN (see CRONUS), who was the Goddess of the Harvest.
Orcus	The Roman name for the King of the Dead. (See HADES, PLUTO.)
Oresitrophos	One of ACTAEON's hounds; the name means "mountain-bred."
Orestes	The son of Agamemnon and Clytemnestra. He avenged his father's murder by killing his mother and her lover.
Oribasos	One of ACTAEON's hounds; the name means "mountain-ranger."
Orion	ARTEMIS's hunter. After she killed him, he was placed in the sky as a constellation.
Orpheus	The greatest mortal musician. He journeyed to the Underworld to find his dead bride, EURYDICE.
Orthia	Another name for ARTEMIS.
Ossa	A mountain in THESSALY once inhabited by centaurs.
Otus	One of twin brothers, both giants, who wanted to prove themselves superior to the gods. ARTEMIS killed them for their presumption by making them accidentally kill each other.
Pachytos	One of ACTAEON's hounds; the name means "thick-skinned."
Paean	The physician to the gods; also, APOLLO as healer.

Pales — The Strengthener of Cattle.

Palladium — The sacred image of ATHENA in TROY that protected the city as long as it was kept there.

Pamphagos — One of ACTAEON's hounds; the name means "ravenous."

Pan — The God of the Goatherds and Shepherds who was part goat and part man.

Pandora — The first woman created by ZEUS; she brought evil into the world.

Panope — One of the sea nymphs.

Paphos — The daughter of the lovers PYGMALION and GALATEA, who gave her name to APHRODITE's favorite city.

Paris — The TROJAN who kidnapped HELEN, starting the Trojan War.

Parthenon — ATHENA's temple in Athens.

Pegasus — The winged horse that sprang from MEDUSA's blood when PERSEUS killed her.

Peitho — The Goddess of Persuasion. She was the daughter of HERMES and APHRODITE.

Pelasgus — The ancestor of the Pelasgian—one of the earliest groups to inhabit the islands and mainland of Greece and Anaholia.

Peleus — ACHILLES' father. He was one of the ARGONAUTS.

Pelias — One of the twin sons of TYRO and POSEIDON.

Pelops	The son of TANTALUS. He was killed by his father, boiled in a cauldron, and served to the gods to eat.
Penates	The Gods of the Hearth and the Guardians of the Storehouse.
Penelope	ODYSSEUS's faithful wife.
Pentheus	King of THEBES who was killed by the Bacchae when he was caught watching their secret rites.
Perdix	The nephew of Daedalus. When Perdix invented the saw and the compass, Daedalus became jealous and tried to kill Perdix. ATHENA saved him by changing him into a partridge.
Pergamos	The holy place of TROY.
Persephone	The Queen of the Underworld and wife of HADES.
Perseus	The hero who killed MEDUSA and was the faithful husband of ANDROMEDA.
Phaedra	ARIADNE's sister and wife of THESEUS. When she fell in love with his son, HIPPOLYTUS, she killed herself.
Phaëthon	The son of APOLLO, whose wish to drive his father's chariot for one day almost led to the end of the world.
Phantasus	Variously, the son or brother of HYPNOS. Phantasus was the God of Dreams of Inanimate Objects.
Phaon	An old boatman to whom APHRODITE gave youth and beauty for ferrying her from Lesbos to Chios.
Philemon	A poor old man who with his wife was blessed by the gods, given a temple to live in, and promised that he would never live alone without her.

Philomela	PROCNE's sister whose husband TEREUS pretended to marry Philomela, then cut out her tongue. The gods turned Philomela into a swallow.
Phineus	A prophet whom ZEUS cursed by having HARPIES defile his food whenever he wanted to eat.
Phobos	The God of Fear. He accompanied ARES into battle.
Phoebe	A TITAN who was the first moon goddess.
Pholus	A centaur-friend of Heracles (HERCULES).
Phrixus	The boy who was rescued from death by the ram with the GOLDEN FLEECE.
Pirene	Famous spring in Corinth.
Pittheus	King of Troezen and the father of THESEUS's mother.
Pluto	The God of the Underworld. (See HADES.)
Plutus	The God of Wealth, a Roman allegorical figure.
Poena	The Roman Goddess of Punishment. The Greeks regarded her an an attendant of NEMESIS.
Pollux	The son of LEDA, who with his brother CASTOR was the Special Protector of Sailors.
Polybus	King of CORINTH, whom OEDIPUS believed was his father.
Polydeuces	Another name for POLLUX.
Polydorus	A son of PRIAM. According to Homer, he was killed by ACHILLES.

Polyidus — A wise seer of Corinth.

Polyxena — HECUBA's daughter who was killed on ACHILLES' grave.

Pomenis — One of ACTAEON's hounds; the name means "leader."

Pomona — The first NUMINA. She was later personified and became the Goddess of Gardens and Orchards.

Pontus — The God of the Deep Sea. He was a son of Mother Earth and the father of the sea god NEREUS.

Porphyrion — A Giant who rebelled against the gods.

Poseidon — The God of the Sea, who was CRONUS's son and ZEUS's brother.

Priam — King of TROY, during the war against the Greeks.

Priapus — The God of Fertility.

Procne — PHILOMELA's sister, who avenged her sister's punishment by killing her own son and feeding him to her husband, TEREUS. The gods changed her into a nightingale.

Procris — The niece of PROCNE and PHILOMELA, who was accidentally killed with her husband's javelin.

Procrustes — A man who tied his victims onto an iron bed and cut or stretched them to fit on the bed. THESEUS killed Procrustes in the same manner.

Proetus — The king of ARGOS.

Prometheus   The Titan whose name means "forethought." He sided with ZEUS in his war with the TITANS.

Proserpine   Another name for PERSEPHONE.

Proteus   The god sometimes said to be POSEIDON's son and sometimes said to be his attendant. Proetus could foretell the future and change his shape, at will.

Psyche   A beautiful maiden who married CUPID and was given immortality.

Psychopompus   Another name for HERMES.

Pterelas   One of ACTAEON's hounds; the name means "winged."

Pygmalion   The sculptor who fell in love with his statue of a woman. APHRODITE brought the sculpture to life, as GALATEA, and the two were married.

Pylades   ORESTES' friend and cousin who helped avenge Agamemnon's murder.

Pylos   NESTOR's home.

Pyramus   The beautiful youth who loved THISBE and killed himself because he thought she was dead. The red fruit of the mulberry is a memorial to the lovers.

Pyrrha   One of two people saved from the Flood that destroyed the world.

Python   A serpent killed by APOLLO.

Remus   One of the twin brothers who founded Rome. As children, they were washed ashore by the Tiber and saved by a she-wolf who fed them her milk. (See ROMULUS.)

Greek and Roman Mythology

Rhea	CRONUS's sister-queen. She was the mother of ZEUS, POSEIDON, HADES, DEMETER, HERA, and HESTIA.
Rhesus	The TROJANS' Thracian ally, whose horses surpassed all mortal ones.
Romulus	REMUS's twin brother who helped found Rome. (See REMUS.)
Salmoneus	A man who pretended to be ZEUS. The god struck him down with a lightning bolt.
Sarpedon	The son of ZEUS and EUROPA. He fought with the TROJANS against the Greeks.
Saturn	The Roman name for CRONUS.
Satyrs	Goat-men who were followers of PAN.
Scamander	The name used by mortals for the great river of TROY (called Xanthos by the gods).
Scheria	The country of the Phaeacians in the Odyssey.
Sciron	A man who made those he captured kneel to wash his feet and then would kick them down to the sea. THESEUS threw him over a precipice.
Scorpio	The scorpion, one of the signs of the Zodiac.
Scylla	A sea nymph whom CIRCE changed into a monster with serpents and dogs' heads coming from her body. Scylla destroyed all sailors who passed her.
Scyros	The island where THESEUS died and ACHILLES disguised himself as a girl.
Selene	The Moon Goddess. Selene was one of ARTEMIS's three forms.

Selli	The people who made bread from acorns in ZEUS's sacred grove.
Semele	DIONYSUS's mother whom Zeus loved.
Sibyl	A prophetess who guided AENEAS to the Underworld.
Sidero	TYRO's maid who married her husband and was killed by Tyro's son, PELIAS.
Sileni	Followers of DIONYSUS and PAN, who were part man and part horse.
Silenus	A jovial fat old man who was always drunk. He was said to be PAN's brother or son.
Simois	One of the rivers of TROY.
Sinis	A man who killed people by fastening them to two pine trees bent down to the ground. When the lashings were cut, his victims were torn limb from limb. THESEUS killed Sinis in the same manner.
Siren	One of the creatures with beautiful voices who lived on an island in the sea and lured sailors to their deaths.
Sirius	The Dog Star in the constellation Canis Major.
Sol	The Roman God of the sun.
Sphinx	The creature shaped like a winged lion with the breast and face of a woman. She beseiged THEBES until OEDIPUS answered her riddle.
Sterope	One of ATLAS's daughters who was placed in the heavens as a star.
Stricta	One of ACTAEON's hounds; the name means "spot."

Styx — The river of the unbreakable oath in the Underworld. Anyone who broke such an oath was banished from the council of the gods and denied nectar and ambrosia.

Sylvanus — One of the NUMINA; the Helper of Plowmen and Woodcutters.

Syracuse — The greatest city of Sicily.

Syrinx — A nymph loved by PAN. Her sister nymphs turned her into a tuft of reeds to save her from him, but he made the reeds into a pipe.

Talus — Last of the Bronze race. Talus was made completely of bronze except for one ankle.

Tantalus — ZEUS's son whom the gods loved. Tantalus hated the gods and served them his son to eat. They discovered his treachery and punished him by putting him in HADES in a pool which drained whenever he tried to drink. They also placed fruit trees above him from which he could never pick fruit.

Tartarus — Another name for the Underworld.

Telamon — The father of AJAX. He was one of the ARGONAUTS.

Telemachus — The son of ODYSSEUS.

Telephus — Heracles' (HERCULES') son. He fought with the Greeks against the TROJANS.

Tempe — A beautiful valley near Mount Olympus.

Tereus — PROCNE's husband. He was changed into a hawk.

Terminus — A NUMINA who was the Guardian of Boundaries.

Thalia	The MUSE of Comedy. She was also one of the three Graces.
Thamyris	A poet who was struck blind when he challenged the MUSES to a contest.
Thea	A TITAN who married her brother Hyperion and gave birth to the sun.
Thebes	The city founded by Cadmus.
Themis	Right or Divine Justice which sat beside ZEUS in OLYMPUS.
Theridamas	One of ACTAEON's hounds; the name means "beast-tamer."
Theron	One of ACTAEON's hounds; the name means "savage-faced."
Theseus	The greatest Athenian hero.
Thespian Lion, The	A lion that ravaged livestock around Mount Cithaeron until Heracles (HERCULES) killed it.
Thessaly	The site of Mount OLYMPUS in northeastern Greece.
Thestius	A king of Calydon who was the father of LEDA and ALTHEA.
Thetis	The sea nymph who was the mother of ACHILLES.
Thisbe	PYRAMUS's lover who killed herself after she found him dead. The red fruit of the mulberry tree is a memorial to them.
Thoös	One of ACTAEON's hounds; the name means "swift."
Thrace	The home of a fierce people in the northeast of Greece.
Tiber	The God of the Tiber River, who instructed AENEAS to go to the site of Rome.

Titan	The elder gods who were huge and strong and ruled over the universe before ZEUS dethroned them.
Tityus	A giant killed by APOLLO and ARTEMIS.
Triton	The Trumpeter of the Sea. He was a son of POSEIDON.

"Ate"—Goddess of Mischief

Trivia   Another name for HECATE.

Trojan   An inhabitant of the city of TROY. (See also TROJAN in Chapter 5).

Troy   A wealthy city on the east end of the Mediterranean, where the Trojan War was fought.

Turnus   The king of the Rutulians who was one of LAVINIA's suitors and consequently battled against AENEAS for her. Turnus lost his life.

Tyche   The Greek name for the Goddess of Fortune.

Tydides   Another name for DIOMEDES.

Tyndaris   The daughter of Tyndareus and LEDA.

Typhoeus   Another name for TYPHON.

Typhon   The monster with a hundred heads whom ZEUS conquered.

Tyro   The woman who bore POSEIDON twin sons, PELIAS and NELEUS.

Ulysses   Another name for ODYSSEUS.

Urania   The MUSE of Astronomy.

Uranis   One of ACTAEON's hounds; the name means "heavenly one."

Uranus   The father of CRONUS, the TITANS, the CYCLOPS, and the Furies.

Venus   The Roman name for APHRODITE.

Vesper	Another name for HESPER.
Vesta	The Roman name for HESTIA.
Victoria	The Roman name for NIKE.
Virbius	The Roman name for HIPPOLYTUS.
Voluptas	The Roman Goddess of Pleasure.
Vulcan	The Roman name for HEPHAESTUS.
Xanthus	The gods' name for Troy's great river.
Zephyr	The God of the West Wind.
Zetes	One of the ARGONAUTS.
Zethus	The twin brother of Amphion. Together, they built a wall around THEBES to fortify it.
Zeus	The Supreme God of the Universe.

"Moses"

CHAPTER 7

Religious Names

All things bright and beautiful,
All creatures great and small,
All things wise and wonderful,
The Lord God made them all.

Cecil Frances Alexander
from *All Things Bright and Beautiful*

This chapter contains names from the world's major religions. Most of the suggestions are from the Judeo-Christian tradition—particularly the Old and New Testaments; but many are derived from Hindu, Buddhist, or Islamic scriptures and related sources.

Aaron	MOSES' brother whose rod became a serpent, when he cast it before Pharaoh. Aaron and his sons became the first priests of the Tabernacle.
Abednego	One of DANIEL's three friends who survived the fiery furnace.
Abel	The son of ADAM and EVE. Abel's brother, CAIN, murdered him.
Abraham	The founder of the Hebrew people.
Absalom	A son of King DAVID who led a revolt against his father.
Adam	The first man created by God.
Agni	The Hindu fire god.
Ahab	The seventh king of the Northern Kingdom who married JEZEBEL. She persuaded him to abandon the worship of God for BAAL, the pagan deity.
Amalek	Esau's grandson who founded a warlike tribe that fought the Israelites.
Amos	A Hebrew prophet.
Ananias	An early Jewish Christian. When he and his wife lied to God, PETER denounced them, and they died.
Andrew	The brother of PETER who was one of the first disciples of Jesus.
Anna	A Hebrew prophetess who worshiped the infant Jesus.
Annas	The High Priest CAIAPHAS's father-in-law. When Jesus appeared before him after his arrest, Annas sent him to Caiaphas.

Antipas	One of Herods sons who ruled Galilee and Perea during Jesus' lifetime. Antipas ordered JOHN THE BAPTIST beheaded.
Archelaus	One of Herod's sons who ruled Judea when JOSEPH (2), MARY (see MARY THE VIRGIN), and Jesus returned from Egypt.
Asenath	The wife of JOSEPH (1) who bore him two sons, Manasseh and EPHRAIM.
Baal	A pagan god worshiped in Phoenicia and Canaan whom some of the Israelites began to worship, angering God.
Barabbas	The robber whom PONTIUS PILATE released instead of Jesus.
Barak	The leader of Israel's forces against the Canaanite forces of King Jabin.
Barnabas	An early convert to Christianity who with PAUL preached the Gospel of Jesus.
Bartholomew	One of the Twelve Apostles, also known as NATHANAEL in one of the Gospels.
Bartimaeus	A blind beggar whose faith in Jesus restored his sight.
Bast	The Egyptian Goddess of Matrimony and Feminine Sensuality. Bast was originally represented as a cat.
Beelzebub	A pagan god whom the Philistines worshiped. He is sometimes identified with Satan.
Belshazzar	The Babylonian ruler for whom DANIEL interpreted the significance of the handwriting on the wall.
Benjamin	The youngest of Jacob's and Rachel's twelve sons.

Religious Names

Boaz	RUTH's second husband to whom she bore a son named Obed.
Brahmə	The supreme Hindu deity, called Creator of the Worlds.
Buddha (Guatama)	The founder of Buddhism, which holds that suffering is inherent in life but that one can rise beyond it by mental and moral self-purification.
Caiaphas	The High Priest, a friend of the Romans, who tried Jesus and then turned Him over to PONTIUS PILATE.
Cain	The first-born son of ADAM and EVE. He killed his brother, ABEL.
Caleb	MOSES' spy who reported on the Canaanites' strength.
Chilion	NAOMI's and ELIMELECH's son.
Chuza	The husband of JOANNA.
Cleopas	One of the two disciples with whom Jesus spoke on the way to Emmaus after the Resurrection.
Cornelius	A Roman centurion who saw a vision and then was baptized by PETER, thus becoming the first Gentile to convert to Christianity.
Cush	A son of HAM named after the land where his descendants lived.
Cyrus	The founder of the Persian Empire who released the Jews and told them to return to Jerusalem.
Dagon	One of the Philistines' pagan gods.
Dalai Lama	The spiritual leader of the Tibetan and Mongolian branch of Buddhism.

Daniel	Israels great prophet whom God delivered from the lions' den.
Darius	The Babylonian king who cast DANIEL to the lions because of his great love for God.
David	The boy who slew the giant GOLIATH and went on to become the greatest of Israel's kings. He built the city of Jerusalem.
Deborah	A prophetess who helped BARAK defeat the Canaanites.
Delilah	SAMSON's love who betrayed him to the Philistines.
Demas	An early Christian who accompanied PAUL during his first Roman imprisonment.
Demetrius	A silversmith who incited a riot against PAUL because the latter's preaching had ruined the man's sale of silver models of the temple of the goddess Diana.
Dinah	A daughter of JACOB and Leah.
Dionysius	An Athenian whom PAUL converted and who became the first bishop of Athens.
Dorcas	Another name for Tabitha, a woman disciple whom PETER raised from the dead.
Drusilla	A daughter of Herod Agrippa I.
Eleazar	One of AARON's sons who became High Priest after his father's death.
Eli	The priest at Shiloh. Hannah brought her son SAMUEL to him.
Elijah	A great prophet of Israel who opposed AHAB and Queen JEZEBEL by fighting against the worship of the BAAL.

Religious Names

Elimelech	NAOMI's husband and father of RUTH's first husband, Mahlon.
Elisabeth	The mother of JOHN THE BAPTIST and a cousin of Mary (see MARY THE VIRGIN), the mother of Jesus.
Elisha	The prophet who succeeded ELIJAH.
Elkanah	The husband of HANNAH who was the father of the prophet SAMUEL.
Enoch	CAIN's eldest son.
Epaenetus	The first Greek convert to Christianity.
Epaphras	An early Christian friend of PAUL.
Ephraim	JOSEPH's second son. Part of Canaan was named for him.
Erastus	One of PAUL's attendants who went as a missionary into Macedonia.
Esau	ISAAC's eldest son who sold his birthright to his brother JACOB for a bowl of lentils.
Esther	A Hebrew orphan girl who married Ahasuerus (Xerxes), the king of Persia, and consequently was able to save her people from persecution.
Eutychus	A young man who fell from a window while listening to PAUL. The apostle restored his life.
Eve	The first woman created by God.
Ezekiel	A major Hebrew prophet.
Ezra	A Hebrew priest and scholar.

Felix — The Roman procurator who tried PAUL.

Gabriel — The archangel who announced the birth of Christ to the Virgin Mary (see MARY THE VIRGIN) and told her what to name Him.

Gad — The son of JACOB and Zilpah who founded one of the Twelve Tribes of Israel.

Gedaliah — The Hebrew governor appointed by NEBUCHADNEZZAR.

Gehazi — The Prophet ELISHA's servant who was cursed with leprosy for betraying his master.

Gershon — One of the three grandsons of JACOB who accompanied him to Eygpt.

Gideon — One of the great judges of Israel, whom God chose to free the Children of Israel from the threat of the Midianites and other hostile tribes.

Goliath — The giant whom DAVID killed.

Habakkuk — A minor Hebrew prophet.

Hagar — SARAH's handmaid. She was the mother of ISHMAEL, who is regarded as the ancestor of the Arabs.

Haggai — A minor Hebrew prophet.

Ham — One of NOAH's sons. Ham is considered the ancestor of all black Africans.

Hamutal — The mother of two kings—Jehoahaz and Zedekiah.

Hannah — The mother of SAMUEL, the judge and prophet.

Hanuman	The monkey god in Hindu mythology.
Heman	A musician and dancer and the grandson of the prophet SAMUEL. Heman sang and played in the Temple during the reign of King DAVID.
Hephzibah	Wife of King HEZEKIAH. The name means "my delight is in her."
Herodias	Herod Antipas's wife who actually was instrumental in the death of JOHN THE BAPTIST.
Hezekiah	A king of Judah who reclaimed some of his nation's lands from the Philistines.
Hilkiah	A high priest who discovered the lost *Book of the Law*, or *Deuteronomy*.
Hophni	ELI's son who, with his brother, died in battle, losing the Ark of the Covenant to the Philistines.
Hosea	A minor prophet.
Hur	A Hebrew who stood by MOSES during the battle with AMALEK.
Ichabod	The grandson of ELI.
Indra	The Hindu Rain God, the King of heaven.
Isaac	ABRAHAM's son whom Abraham almost sacrificed to God to prove his faith. Isaac married REBEKAH, and they had two sons, ESAU and JACOB.
Isaiah	Generally regarded as the greatest Hebrew prophet.
Ishmael	Abraham's son by HAGAR, his wife's handmaid. Ishmael founded a great nation of people in Arabia, where the Muslims revere him.

Israel	The name given to JACOB by an angel, which the Twelve Hebrew Tribes later adopted.
Jacob	Son of ISAAC and REBEKAH, who wrestled with the angel of the Lord and consequently was named ISRAEL.
Jambavat	The Hindu King of the Bears.
James	(1) The son of Alphaeus who became one of the Twelve Apostles. (2) The Apostle who was the son of ZEBEDEE and the brother of JOHN.
Jehoshaphat	One of JUDAH's greatest kings, who tried to abolish paganism and who was a great military leader.
Jeremiah	A major Hebrew prophet.
Jesse	King DAVID's father.
Jezebel	The evil queen married to King AHAB. She persecuted the Israelites until chariot horses trampled her to death.
Joanna	One of Jesus' earliest followers.
Job	A man who suffered a long series of great miseries. His name has become synonymous with patience.
John	One of the Twelve Apostles. He is considered the author of *Revelations* and the *Gospel of John.*
John the Baptist	Jesus' forerunner.

Religious Names

Jonah	The Hebrew prophet who was swallowed by a whale because he did not want to go to Nineveh to preach. He repented and went to Nineveh.
Joseph	(1) One of JACOB's and RACHEL's sons. Joseph's jealous brothers sold him as a slave into Egypt. (2) The husband of Mary (see MARY THE VIRGIN), the mother of Jesus.
Joshua	An Israelite who after MOSES' death led his people in their first conquests in Canaan.
Judah	JACOB's fourth son who founded the largest of the Twelve Tribes of Israel.
Judas Iscariot	The Apostle who betrayed Jesus to His enemies.
Jude	The son of Mary (see MARY THE VIRGIN) and JOSEPH, thus believed by some to be a brother of Jesus.
Kama	The Hindu God of Love.
Kasmir (or Katmir or Kitmir)	The dog, according to Muslim tradition, that was one of the animals Mohammed admitted to Paradise.
Krishna	An incarnation of VISHNU.
Lazarus	Jesus' friend and the brother of MARTHA and MARY OF BETHANY. Jesus raised Lazarus from the dead.
Levi	One of JACOB's sons. Levi founded one of the Twelve Tribes of Israel.
Lot	ABRAHAM's nephew whom God saved, along with his family, from the destruction of Sodom.

Lucifer	The light-bearer; the star that brings in the day (the morning star). Originally an archangel, Lucifer led a rebellion, was cast out of heaven, and became identified with the Devil.
Luke	An early Christian who accompanied PAUL on two of his missionary journeys. The third gospel is attributed to Luke.
Lydia	A wealthy woman who was PAUL's first European convert.
Malachi	A prophet of Israel.
Mark	One of the Evangelists. He is considered the author of the *Gospel of Mark*.
Martha	The sister of LAZARUS and MARY OF BETHANY.
Mary Magdalene	A woman who was one of Jesus' devoted followers. She was one of the two women who discovered Jesus' empty tomb.
Mary of Bethany	The sister of MARTHA and LAZARUS, who anointed Jesus in Simon the Leper's house.
Mary the Virgin	The mother of Jesus and wife of JOSEPH.
Matthew	One of the Twelve Apostles whose original name was LEVI. The *Gospel of Matthew* is ascribed to him.
Matthias	The disciple chosen to take the place of JUDAS.
Mecca	The birthpalace of MOHAMMED in Saudi Arabia and the Islamic holy city.
Meshach	One of DANIEL's three companions who survived the fiery furnace.

Religious Names

Methuselah	A Biblical figure who was renowned for his longevity.
Meuzza	MOHAMMED's beloved cat. She was one of the animals admitted to Islamic Paradise.
Micah	A minor Hebrew prophet.
Miriam	MOSES and AARON's sister who became a prophetess.
Mohammed	The founder of the Islamic religion.
Moses	The Hebrew prophet who led the Israelites out of Egypt and who received the Ten Commandments from God.
Naomi	The mother-in-law of RUTH.
Nathanael	One of the Twelve Apostles, known as BARTHOLOMEW in the first three Gospels.
Nebuchadnezzar	A powerful king of Babylon who invaded Israel several times, carrying its people into bondage and razing Jerusalem and the holy Temple.
Nicodemus	A Pharisee who defended Jesus at one of His trials, and buried Him after the Crucifixion.
Noah	The builder of the ark who saved himself, his family, and two of each of the world's animals from the Flood.
Obadiah	A minor prophet.
Obed	The grandfather of King DAVID.

Paul	The first Christian missionary who had persecuted Christians until he saw a vision on the road to Damascus.
Peter	The Apostle who as a fisherman had been called SIMON (THE CANAANITE). Jesus changed his name to Peter, meaning "rock."
Philip	One of the Twelve Apostles.
Pontius Pilate	The Roman procurator of Judea who tried and condemned Jesus.
Ra	The Eygptian God of the Sun.
Rachel	The wife of JACOB's and mother of his sons, JOSEPH and BENJAMIN.
Rama	The Hindu king who was the son of Vishnu, his incarnation on earth.
Ravan	The Hindu demon king.
Rebekah	The wife of ABRAHAM's son ISAAC and mother of his sons, ESAU and JACOB.
Reuben	JACOB's first son who founded one of the Twelve Tribes of Israel.
Ruth	The young woman whose story is told in the Old Testament *Book of Ruth*. She was the great-grandmother of King DAVID.
Samson	The strongest man in the Bible who received his strength from his long hair. His love, DELILAH, betrayed him.
Samuel	A prophet and judge of Israel who delivered the Israelites at Mizpah from Philistine oppression and who anointed SAUL as the first king of Israel.

Religious Names

Sarah	The wife of ABRAHAM.
Sarama	The great god INDRA's watchdog and messenger in Hindu mythology.
Sarameyau	SARAMA's savage twin sons in Hindu mythology, who guided the souls of the dead to their final resting place.
Saraswati	The Hindu Goddess of Speech.
Saul	The first king of Israel.
Seth	The third son of ADAM and EVE.
Shadrach	One of DANIEL's three companions who survived the fiery furnace.
Sheba (Queen of)	The wealthy queen who visited King SOLOMON.
Shiva	The great Hindu god whose third eye will destroy the world.
Simeon	A son of JACOB and LEAH, who founded one of the Twelve Tribes of Israel.
Simon (the Canaanite)	One of the Twelve Apostles.
Simon of Cyrene	The man who carried the cross for Jesus.
Sita	RAMA's wife, the ideal Hindu woman.
Solomon	King DAVID's son who became the third king of Israel and built the first Temple.
Stephen	An early Christian. He was stoned to death for his beliefs, thereby becoming the first Christian martyr.

Thaddaeus	One of the Twelve Apostles. He is also called Jude and Lebbaeus.
Thomas	The Apostle known as "doubting Thomas" because he would not believe in the Resurrection until he saw Jesus' wounds.
Timothy	PAUL's friend and companion.
Titus	PAUL's Greek assistant and companion, who was converted by him.
Tobit's Dog	(1) One of the animals placed in Islamic Paradise. (2) The dog who appears in the *Book of Tobit* in the Apocrypha to the Bible.
Varuna	The Hindu God of the Waters.
Vayu	The Hindu God of the Wind.
Vishnu	The great Hindu god who preserves the three worlds.
Yama	The Hindu God of Death.
Zacharias	A priest who was the father of JOHN THE BAPTIST.
Zebedee	The father of the two apostles JAMES and JOHN.
Zechariah (or Zachariah)	A priest and minor Hebrew prophet whose visions and teachings appear in the Old Testament that bears his name.
Zephaniah	A minor prophet of Israel whose teachings appear in the Old Testament named for him.
Zoroaster	A Persian religious teacher, the founder of the Zoroastrian religion.

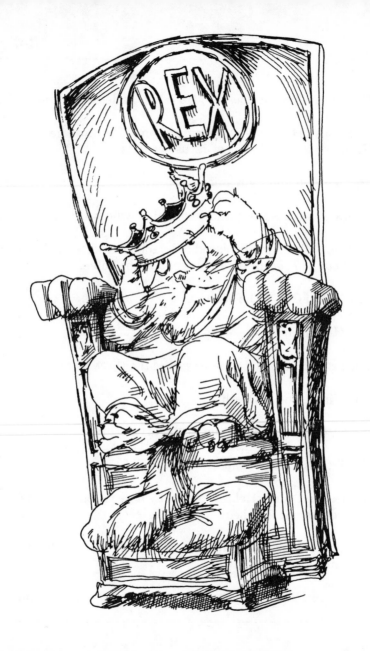

CHAPTER 8

Royalty and Titles

I'll call the Hamlet,
King, father, Royal Dane: Oh, answer me!

William Shakespeare
from *Hamlet*

No better way exists to exalt your pet and show your high esteem than by giving it a prestigious title. Most of the names in this section are royal designations, but quite a few are military or civil.

Royalty and Titles

Admiral	Captain	Corporal	Czar (Tsar)
Ambassador	Chief	Counselor	Czarina
Baron	Colonel	Count	(Tsarina)
Baroness	Commander	Countess	Detective

"Pasha"

Duchess	Khan	Mistress	Queen/Queenie
Duke	King	Officer	Representative
Earl	Lady	Pasha	Rex
Emperor	Lieutenant	Patriarch	Sergeant
Empress	Lord	Pharaoh	Secretary
General	Majesty	Premier	Senator
Governor	Major	President	Shah
Highness	Master	Prime Minister	Sheik
Inspector	Matriarch	Prince	Shogun
Judge	Mayor	Princess	Squire
Kaiser	Midshipman		

"McDuff"

CHAPTER 9

Foreign Words and Names

A man who is ignorant of foreign languages is ignorant of his own.

Johann von Goethe

If you have a flair for the exotic, or simply want to impress your friends with your multilingual skills, then the names in this chapter will intrigue you and possibly prompt you to open a foreign language dictionary. Your best choice is a pleasant sounding word, preferably one you can pronounce correctly, and one with a translation that appropriately fits your pet. For instance, be careful not to embarrass yourself and your black cat by naming him Amarillo, the Spanish word for "yellow"!

Foreign Words and Names

Agape	Latin for word meaning "love."
Aloha	Hawaiian word for "hello" or "goodbye."
Amarillo (2)	Spanish for "yellow." Use Amarillo for a male and Amarilla for a female.
Amigo(a)	Spanish word meaning "friend." Use Amigo for a male and Amiga for a female.
Amore	Italian for "love."
Astra	Latin for "star."
Azul	Spanish for "blue."
Beau/Belle	French for "handsome/beautiful."
Bébé	French for "baby."
Beeren	German for "berries."
Bianca Pinjarra	Some of the crown jewels of England.
Bianco(a)	Italian for "white." Use Bianco for a male and Bianca for a female.
Bier	German word for "beer."
Bijou	French for "jewel."
Blanco(a)	Spanish for "white." Use Blanco for a male and Blanca for a female.

Blanquito(a)	Spanish for "little white one." Use Blanquito for a male and Blanquita for a female.
Bleu	French for "blue."
Bonito(a)	Spanish for "pretty." Use Bonito for a male and Bonita for a female.
Canela	Spanish for "cinnamon."
Caro	Italian for "dear."
Celia	"Little heavenly one."
Chansu	Japanese for "chance."
Chat	French for "cat."
Chico	Spanish for "young man."
Chien	French for "dog."
Chiquita	Spanish for "little girl."
Coeur	French for "heart."
Concha	Spanish for "shell."
Diablo	Spanish for "devil."
Dolce	Italian for "sweet."

Foreign Words and Names

Dono	Italian for "gift."
Faux Pas	French for "a social blunder."
Felice	Italian for "happy."
Feliz	Spanish for "happy."
Feo	Spanish for "ugly."
Fiesta	Spanish for "party."
Flavo	Italian for "fair or blonde."
Fraulein	German for "young woman."
Freida	A German name for a female.
Frieden	German for "peace."
Frijol	Spanish for "bean."
Fritz	A German name for a male.
Gato (2)	Spanish for "cat." Use Gato for a male and Gata for a female.
Greta	A German name for a female.
Gretchen	A German name for a female.
Gretel	A German name for a female.

Gris	Spanish for "gray."
Hans	A German name for a male.
Heidi	A German name for a female.
Heinrich	A German name for a male; it translates as "Henry."
Hombre	Spanish for "man."
Hummel	A German name for a male.
Ilsa	A German name for a female.
José	A Spanish name for a male.
Kannika	"Jasminelike blossom" in Japanese.
Katarina (Katrina)	A Russian name for a female.
Kline	German for "small."
Kut	The Egyptian name for the male cat.
Kutta	The Egyptian name for the female cat.
Laddie	Scottish for "young man."
Lassie	Scottish for "young woman."
Lieb	German for "dear."

Foreign Words and Names

Liesel	A German name for a female.
Linda	Spanish for "pretty."
Luna	Spanish for "moon."
Madame	French for "Mrs. or Madam."
Mademoiselle	French for "Miss."
Mar	Spanish for "sea."
Marta	A German name for a female.
McCloud	A Scottish name.
McDuff	A Scottish name.
McMurphy	A Scottish name.
McTavish	A Scottish name.
Mesa	Spanish for "table."
Messieur	French for "mister."
Mi	Spanish for "my."
Misha	A Russian name for a male.
Monique	A French name for a female.

Muñeca	Spanish for "doll."
Natasha	A Russian name for a female.
Nicole	A French name for a female.
Octavia/n	A Latin name for a female/male.
Omar	A Middle Eastern name.
Oso(a)	Spanish for "bear." Use Oso for a male and Osa for a female.
Paco	A Spanish name for a male.
Pancho	A Spanish name for a male.
Pepe	A Spanish name for a male.
Perro (a)	Spanish for "dog." Use Perro for a male and Perra for a female.
Poco	Spanish for "little."
Renée	A French name.
Rojo(a)	Spanish for "red." Use Rojo for a male and Roja for a female.
Rosita	A Spanish name for a female.
Sasha	A Russian name.
Schnell	German for "fast" or "quick."

Foreign Words and Names

Schotzie   A German name.

Simba   African for "lion."

Sayonara   Japanese for "goodbye."

Som Phong   Tai word meaning "like one's ancestors."

Suki   A Japanese name.

Summa   Latin for "the most."

Sushi   Japanese for "raw fish."

Tanya   A Russian name for a female.

Tasha   A Russian name for a female. (Short for Natasha.)

Tigre (a)   Spanish for "tiger." Use Tigre for a male and Tigra for a female.

Toro   Spanish for "bull."

Toutou   French for "doggie."

Trinka   A German name for a female. (Short for Katrinka.)

Wolfgang   A German name for a male.

"Sushi"

"Puss in Boots"

CHAPTER 10

Literature and Art

Ghastly grim and ancient Raven wandering
from the nightly shore—
Tell me what thy lordly name is on the
Night's Plutonian shore!
Quoth the raven, "Nevermore."

Edgar Allan Poe
from *The Raven*

Some of the most memorable animals are those that appear in literature and art. This chapter includes many of those animals, particularly dogs and cats, as well as a few famous human literary and artistic characters.

Literature and Art

Agatha Christie	The famous twentieth century mystery writer.
Alidoro	A mastiff in Carlos Collodi's (Lorenzini) *Pinocchio* (1883). Pinocchio saved Alidoro from drowning; in return Alidoro rescued the puppet from being fried like a fish when coated with flour.
Appollinaris	A cat that belonged to Mark Twain.
Aristophanes	A Greek comedy writer during the last half of the fifth and first half of the fourth centuries B.C. He refers to the myths in his works.
Ashley	The master of Twelve Oaks in Margaret Mitchell's classic novel *Gone With the Wind*. (1936).
Banshee	A female spirit in Gaelic folklore whose appearance or wailing warns a family of the approaching death of one of its members.
Barge	In *The Fireside Book of Dog Stories* (1943), James Thurber tells of Barge, a watchdog who lived with a family in Columbus, Ohio. Barge took to drinking and neglected his duties until he came home one day and found that burglars had broken into his house. In despair and shame, Barge jumped out of a window and killed himself.
Baron	A dachshund written by Louis J. Camuti, in *Park Avenue Vet.*
Basket	Gertrude Stein's two dogs of the same name. They are described in works that Stein wrote in France during the period of the German occupation (1940–1945).
Ben	A dog described by Maxwell Knight, in *My Pet Friends*.

Beowulf — The hero of the Anglo-Saxon epic poem *Beowulf.*

Big Red — The $7,000 Irish setter in Jim Kjelgaard's *Big Red* (1945). Big Red ruined his chances to be a show dog when he injured himself fighting a wolverine and a bear, thereby saving his master Danny Pickett.

Bilbo Baggins — One of the hobbits in J. R. Tolkien's novels.

Bion — An Alexandrian pastoral poet who wrote of the myths, around 250 B.C.

Blackie — A black spaniel that was Ernest Hemingway's companion for 12 years.

Blanche — One of the dogs that does not appear on stage but is mentioned in act 3, scene 6 of Shakespeare's play *King Lear* (1608).

Bodger — The old bull terrier in Sheila Burnford's *The Incredible Journey* (1961). Bodger was one of the three pets who faced tremendous hardships while traveling home through the Canadian wilderness.

Brownie — The female Irish setter owned by T. H. White, the author of *The Once and Future King* (1958). White described his love for Brownie in his letters to David Garnett.

Buck — The large, powerful, mix-breed dog in Jack London's *The Call of the Wild.* Stolen from his home in California to be sold as a sled dog in Alaska, Buck was "beaten but not broken." He eventually joined a pack of wolves who signaled their acceptance of Buck by sniffing noses and howling at the moon.

Bull's-eye — The white shaggy mutt in Charles Dickens's *Oliver Twist* (1839). Bull's-eye belonged to the murderer, Bill Sikes, and had as unpleasant a disposition as his owner.

Bunyan (Paul)   The mythical lumberjack hero of the American West.

Cadpig   The smallest and prettiest of Pongo's fifteen puppies in Dodie Smith's *The Hundred and One Dalmatians* (1956). Cadpig's favorite pastime is watching television.

Catarina   A large tortoiseshell cat that belonged to Edgar Allan Poe and his wife Virginia. Catarina would lie on Virginia to keep her warm when Virginia was bedridden.

Catfish   Columnist Lewis Grizzard's dog who, as Grizzard reports in his column, liked to drink out of the toilet.

Charley   The large French poodle that accompanied John Steinbeck on his trip through the United States in the 1960s. Steinbeck recalls their adventures in *Travels with Charley* in which Charley is described as being his ambassador when meeting strange people.

Chaucer (Geoffrey)   The greatest English poet of the Middle Ages who is best known for his classic, *The Canterbury Tales*.

Cheshire Cat, The   The famous grinning cat whom Alice encounters during her journey in *Alice's Adventures in Wonderland* (1865) by Lewis Carroll. (See also *Cheshire Cat* in Chapter 11.)

Cinderella   The girl who marries Prince Charming in the well-known fairy tale *Cinderella*.

Clarissa   A dog in James Thurber's "How to Name A Dog."

Columbine   A stock character in early Italian comedy and pantomime. Columbine was the daughter of Pantaloon and the sweetheart of HARLEQUIN.

Cotton-Tail
The brother of Flopsy and Mopsy. These three were the "good little bunnies [who] went down to the lane to gather blackberries," from Beatrix Potter's *The Tale of Peter Rabbit*.

Dante (Alighieri)
One of the greatest medieval poets. Dante's major literary work was *The Divine Comedy*.

Dash
A mongrel dog that belonged to writer Charles Lamb. Dash had once belonged to poet Thomas Hood. Lamb wrote about Dash's "crazy" behavior, which included the ability to stand on his hind legs.

Dickens (Charles)
One of the most popular English novelists who criticized the wealthy and corrupt in nineteenth century England.

Digit
A gorilla in the book *Gorillas in the Mist* by Diane Fosse (1983). He got his name from the fourth and fifth digits of his hand, which were webbed.

Dinah
Alice's cat, who was left behind when Alice fell down the rabbit-hole in Lewis Carroll's *Alice's Adventures in Wonderland* (1865).

Diogenes
The brutish dog that adored his owner, Florence Dombey, in Charles Dickens's *Dombey and Son* (1848).

Don Juan
One of the most famous literary figures in medieval legends. Don Juan has appeared in the works of Byron, Shaw, Molière, and Mozart.

Dr. Watson
Sherlock Holmes's companion and the narrator of Sir Arthur Conan Doyle's (1859–1930) mystery books.

Duke
Penrod Schofield's dog. A scraggly, but faithful, companion in Booth Tarkington's *Penrod* (1914). (See also *Duke* in Chapter 5.)

El Dorado	The fictitious kingdom of untold wealth on the Amazon River for which Spanish and English explorers searched.
Euripides	A Greek tragic poet of the fifth century B.C., who wrote plays based on myths.
Feathers	Carl van Vechten's cat whose behavior he discussed in *The Tiger in the House* (1920).
Flopsy	One of the "good little bunnies" in Beatrix Potter's stories. (See COTTON-TAIL.)
Flossy	English writer Anne Brontë's fat little black and white spaniel.
Flush	Elizabeth Barrett Browning's red cocker spaniel. Elizabeth was holding Flush when she met Robert in Hodgson's Bookshop in 1846.
Fortitude	One of two lions whose statues guard the Fifth Avenue entrance to the main building of the New York Public Library . (See PATIENCE.)
Foss	Edward Lear's beloved tomcat for whom he created "The Heraldic Blazon of Foss the Cat," published in *Nonsense Songs, Stories, Botany and Alphabets*.
Fu Manchu	The villain in Sax Rohmer novels.
Gatsby (Jay)	A racketeer of the 1920s in F. Scott Fitzgerald's classic novel *The Great Gatsby* (1925).
Gipsy	The cat who left home to become an alley cat, in Booth Tarkington's *Penrod and Sam*.

Grimalkin
: The demon spirit in the form of a cat mentioned by the First Witch in Shakespeare's *Macbeth* (1605).

Guinevere
: King Arthur's wife in the stories of King Arthur and the Round Table.

Harlequin
: A clown in early Italian comedy and pantomime. Harlequin's tight-fitting costume has alternating patches of contrasting colors.

Heidi
: The heroine of *Heidi* by Johanna Spyri (1827–1901).

Herodotus
: The first historian of Europe. He refers to the myths in his works.

Hinse
: The cat that belonged to the poet and novelist Sir Walter Scott of Edinburgh (1771–1832).

Homer
: The blind poet who wrote of the Greek myths in the *Iliad* and *The Odyssey*.

Hound of the Baskervilles, The
: The ghostly black hound that dwelt on the moors of Dartmoor and terrorized the Baskerville family in Sir Arthur Conan Doyle's *The Hound of the Baskervilles* (1902).

Jeannie
: A Scotty that appears in *Thurber's Dogs* (1955).

Jennie
: The discontented Sealyham terrier that became the star of the World Mother Goose Theatre in Maurice Sendak's *Higglety Pigglety Pop! or There Must Be More to Life* (1967).

Jip
: (1) Dora Spenlow's small black spaniel who liked to walk on the dinner table in Charles Dickens's *David Copperfield* (1850). (2) The dog with an acute sense of smell that helped save a man stranded on an island in Hugh Lofting's *The Story of Doctor Dolittle* (1920).

Juliet	One of the star-crossed lovers in Shakespeare's *Romeo and Juliet* (1594–95).
Keeper	Emily Brontë's mastiff. When his mistress died, Keeper followed the coffin in the funeral procession and slept for nights at the door of her empty room.
Kiche	The she-wolf that whelped WHITE FANG in Jack London's *White Fang* (1906).
King Arthur	The legendary king of the Britons who restored order and peace in his kingdom. King Arthur's story is told in various literary works.
Lad	The thoroughbred collie who accomplished amazing deeds in Albert Payson Terhune's *Lad: A Dog* (1919). Terhune based Lad on his own collie, Sunnybank Lad.
Lady Godiva	The wife of Loefric, Earl of Mercia and Lord of Coventry. She rode naked through the town to get her husband to lower heavy taxes on the people. (c.1040–1080).
Lancelot	Sir Lancelot du Lac, the best of King Arthur's knights who loved Arthur's wife GUINEVERE in the stories of King Arthur and the Round Table.
Lassie	The collie in Eric Knight's pre-World War II short story "Lassie Come Home" (1938), who has since become a symbol of loyalty and dignity.
Lion of Lucerne, The (Lowendenkmal)	A statue of a dying lion erected in Lucerne's Glacier Garden to commemorate the Swiss Guards who were killed defending Louis XVI during the French Revolution.
Lobo	The "King of Currumpaw," leader of a pack of wolves that attacked cattle in New Mexico. Ernest Thompson Seton wrote of his attempts to capture Lobo in *Wild Animals I Have Known* (1898). Seton finally succeeded by luring the wolf with the dead body of his mate, Blanca. (See BLANCA.)

Lucian A second century A.D. Greek writer who satirized the gods.

Macavity The ginger cat that mysteriously disappears whenever anything turns up missing in "Macavity: the Mystery Cat" from *Old Possum's Book of Practical Cats* (1939) by T. S. Eliot.

Max A dachshund that is mentioned by Matthew Arnold in the elegy "Poor Matthias" (1882). See also MORITZ.

Merrylegs Jupe's performing circus dog in Charles Dickens's *Hard Times* (1854) who disappeared with his owner, only to return to the circus alone, lame, and almost blind.

Minnaloushe A black cat that is the subject of three verses in William Butler Yeats's *The Cat and the Moon* (1919).

Miss Muffet The girl frightened by a spider in the popular nursery rhyme.

Mistigris Madame Vauquer's cat in Honoré de Balzac's *Le Père Goriot* (1835).

Mittens The kitten who laughed so hard she fell off the wall in Beatrix Potter's *The Tale of Tom Kitten*.

Mona Lisa Leonardo Da Vinci's famous painting of the woman with the mysterious smile.

Monsieur Tibault The cat that conducted a symphony orchestra with his tail in Stephen Vincent Benét's *The King of the Cats* (1929).

Moppet One of the two kittens that "trod upon their pinafores and fell on their noses, " in Beatrix Potter's *The Tale of Tom Kitten*.

Mopsy	One of the "good little bunnies" in Beatrix Potter's stories. (See COTTON-TAIL.)
Moritz	From *Max and Moritz,* the German classic by Wilhelm Busch. The names designate a pair of mischief-makers.
Morris	The famous finicky, striped tomcat of 9-Lives Cat Food commercials whose biography was written by Mary Daniels in 1974.
Mouschi	A cat that belonged to Ann Frank as described in *Diary of a Young Girl.*
Muggs	(1) The ferocious Airedale in James Thurber's "The Dog That Bit People" from *My Life and Hard Times* (1933). (2) One of James Thurber's dogs included in his book, *Thurber's Dogs* (1955).
Music	The female greyhound described by William Wordsworth in the poem, "Incident Characteristic of a Favorite Dog" (1805). Music, who belonged to Mrs. Wordsworth's brother, tried desperately to save her friend Dart who had fallen through the ice on a lake. As she was breaking away the ice with her paws, Wordsworth described the scene: " . . . For herself she hath no fears Him alone she sees and hears."
Mutt	An amusing, black and white mongrel in Farley Mowat's *The Dog Who Wouldn't Be* (1957).
Nana	The Newfoundland dog that is the Darling children's nurse in J. M. Barrie's *Peter Pan* (1904).
Nero	Jane Welsh Carlyle's white terrier, part Maltese and part mongrel, who one day jumped from the library window, knocking himself senseless. Virginia Woolf relates the incident, claiming that perhaps the dog was attempting suicide, in *Flush* (1933).

Nox	The big black retriever whose behavior helped Father Brown solve Colonel Druce's murder in G. K. Chesterton's "The Oracle of the Dog" from *The Incredulity of Father Brown* (1926).
Old Bob	The gray collie that was an award-winning sheepherder in *Bob, Son of Battle* (1898) by Alfred Ollivant.
Old Yeller	The rugged, stray yellow-gold dog who was adopted in Fred Gipson's *Old Yeller,* a novel about the Texas hill country in the frontier days of the 1860s. Old Yeller's name had a double meaning: the color of his hair coat and the yelling sounds he made.
Oliver (Twist)	The orphan in Charles Dickens's novel *Oliver Twist* (1837–39).
Ovid	A Latin narrative poet who retold almost all of the stories of classical mythology.
Patience	One of two lions whose statues guard the Fifth Avenue entrance to the main building of the New York Public Library. (See FORTITUDE.)
Pepper	The names of three of Dandie Dinmont's six terriers (the other three were named MUSTARD) in Sir Walter Scott's *Guy Mannering* (1815).
Peter Rabbit	The mischievous little rabbit in Beatrix Potter's *The Tale of Peter Rabbit*. When Peter was hiding under a flower pot, he sneezed and was discovered by Mr. McGregor.
Pindar	Greece's greatest lyric poet who alludes to the myths in all his poems.
Pinocchio	The puppet whose nose grew when he lied in *Pinocchio* (1883) by Carlos Collodi (Lorenzini).

Professor Moriarity	The arch enemy of Sherlock Holmes in Sir Arthur Conan Doyle's (1859–1930), mystery books.
Puss in Boots	The clever cat that was the sole inheritance a poor boy received from his father. The cat, who asked only for a pair of boots, tricked an ogre by challenging him to turn himself into a mouse. The cat ate the ogre and his master took over the ogre's lands and castle.
Rab	The powerful dog in Dr. John Brown's *Rab and His Friends* that kept a vigil at the bedside of his owner Ailie during her illness and subsequent death.
Raksha	The Mother Wolf that raised Mowgli in Rudyard Kipling's *The Jungle Book* (1894).
Remus (Uncle)	The narrator of a series of stories by Joel Chandler Harris (1848–1908). Uncle Remus was a former slave who became a beloved family servant and who entertains a young boy by telling him animal stories.
Rhett	The irreverent Southerner who becomes Scarlet's third husband in Margaret Mitchell's *Gone With the Wind* (1936).
Rikki-Tikki-Tavi	The title character in Rudyard Kipling's short story about a mongoose that fights cobras.
Romeo	One of the star-crossed lovers in Shakespeare's *Romeo and Juliet* (1594–95).
Rover	The collie that was President Lyndon Johnson's first dog.
Rum Tum Tugger	A fictional cat in *Old Possum's Book of Practical Cats* by T. S. Eliot (1939).
Savage Sam	Old Yeller's son in Fred Gipson's novel *Savage Sam* (1962).

Scarlet   The heroine of Margaret Mitchell's *Gone With the Wind* (1936).

Schuster   See SIMON.

Selima   Horace Walpole's tabby cat who was immortalized in a poem by Thomas
                          Gray. Selima drowned in a goldfish bowl white trying to catch a fish.
                          (Indeed, "curiosity killed the cat."!)

Sergeant Murphy   The brown dog that is a motorcycle-riding police officer in Richard Scarry's
                          picture books.

Shakespeare   The English playwright who is known as history's greatest dramatist and
(William)   the best English-language poet.

Shep   Shep, a Collie that took care of a flock of sheep in New York City's Central
                          Park, is described in an early twentieth-century story.

Sherlock Holmes   The famous detective in Sir Arthur Conan Doyle's (1859–1930) books.

Shimbleshanks   One of the cats in *Old Possum's Book of Practial Cats* by T. S. Eliot (1939).

Simon   Co-founder of Simon & Schuster, a major New York publisher.

Simpkin   The tailor's cat in Beatrix Potter's *The Tailor of Gloucester* (1903).

Sinbad (the Sailor)   The sailor whose adventures include battling monsters in *The Arabian
                          Nights.*

Sneakers   A cat about whom Margaret Wise Brown wrote in her *Seven Stories About a
                          Cat Named Sneakers.*

Literature and Art

Sophocles	A Greek playwright who wrote about the myths.
Sounder	The sharecropper's faithful dog with the resonant voice in William H. Armstrong's *Sounder* (1969).
Sour Mash	One of Mark Twain's several feline pets.
Stephen King	A contemporary author of horror books, including *Carrie* and *The Shining*.
Stumpy	The big brown dog in Beatrix Potter's *The Tale of Little Pig Robinson* (1930).
Sweetheart	A dog referred to in Act 3, Scene 6 of Shakespeare's *King Lear* (1608).
Tabitha (Tabby)	A Siamese cat in *One Kitten Too Many* by Bianco Bradbury. Tabitha was called Tabby for short.
Tabitha Twitchit	The mother cat that was a shrewd businesswoman in Beatrix Potter's books.
Tailspin	The cat that was born on the moon in *Space Cat* by Ruthven Todd.
Tao	The male Siamese cat in *The Incredible Journey* (1961) by Sheila Burnford.
Tara	The O'Hara family's plantation in Margaret Mitchell's classic novel, *Gone With the Wind* (1936).
Tessa	A dog that belonged to author James Thurber.
Theocritus	An Alexandrian pastoral poet who wrote of the gods.

Tiger · The cat that played with KEEPER, the dog, in the household of Emily and Charlotte Brontë. (See also TIGER in Chapter 5.)

Tigger · The bouncy tiger in A. A. Milne's *The House at Pooh Corner* (1928).

Tinkerbell · The tiny fairy in *Peter Pan* (1904) by J. M. Barrie.

Toby · (1) A puppet dog in the Punch and Judy shows. (2) The ugly part spaniel who assists Sherlock Holmes and Dr. Watson in Sir Arthur Conan Doyle's *The Sign of Four* (1890).

Tom Kitten · The naughty kitten in Beatrix Potter's *The Tale of Tom Kitten* who was so fat his buttons burst off his clothes. He later lost his clothes, which were found by some ducks who wore them.

Tom Quartz · A kitten that President Theodore Roosevelt named for the fictional cat Tom Quartz in Mark Twain's book *Roughing It* (1872).

Toto · The dog that journeys with Dorothy in L. Frank Baum's *The Wonderful Wizard of Oz* (1900).

Tray · The dog in Thomas Campbell's poem "The Harper."

Virgil · A Roman poet who wrote of the myths.

William · (1) Charles Dickens's (1812–1870) dear white cat, which he renamed Williamina when she had kittens. (2) The egotistical cat obsessed with his own name in James Thurber's "The Cat in the Lifeboat" from *Further Fables for Our Time* (1956).

Winnie-the-Pooh | The opinionated but delightful hero of A. A. Milne's stories about a teddy bear and his friends.

Wolf | The dog that accompanied Rip Van Winkle on the day that he fell asleep for 20 years (from Washington Irving's story of the same name).

Zoroaster | One of Mark Twain's several cats.

CHAPTER 11

Screen and Television

The play's the thing . . . !

William Shakespeare
from *Hamlet*

Who's the star of your household? Perhaps it's "Tonto," "Dracula," "Lassie," or maybe "Morris." Take your pick. But be careful; sometimes animals assume the characteristics of their namesakes. (Beware of "Pepe Le Pew.")

Amos	The character played by Alvin Childress on the television show "Amos 'n' Andy."
Andy	The character played by Spencer Williams on the television show "Amos 'n' Andy."
Apollo	One of the two Doberman pinschers owned by Robbin Masters on the television series "Magnum P.I." (See ZEUS.)
Arnold	The pet pig in the television series "Green Acres" starring Eddie Albert and Eva Gabor.
Arthur	The drunken millionaire played by Dudley Moore in the movie *Arthur*.
Asta	The wirehaired fox terrier in the television series "The Thin Man." The Humane Association gave Asta two Patsy Awards for performing animals.
B. J. Honneycut	Hawkeye's buddy on the television series "M*A*S*H."
Bagheera	The black panther in the Walt Disney movie *The Jungle Book* (1966).
Baloo	The bear in Walt Disney's movie *The Jungle Book* (1966).
Bam Bam	Barney and Betty Rubble's son in Hanna-Barbera's animated television cartoon "The Flintstones."
Bambi	The fawn in Walt Disney's animated movie *Bambi* (1942).
Barnaby Jones	The private eye played by Buddy Ebsen in the television series "Barnaby Jones."

Barney (Rubble) The best friend of Fred Flintstone in Hanna-Barbera's animated television cartoon "The Flintstones."

Bart Maverick One of the brothers, played by Jack Kelly, living in the frontier west in the television series "Maverick."

Bashful One of the Seven Dwarfs in the Walt Disney movie *Snow White and the Seven Dwarfs* (1937).

Batman Batman first appeared in *Detective Comics* in May 1939. In the spring of 1940, *Batman Comics* evolved. The Mutual Radio Network also featured the voices of Batman and Robin during the 1940s. The ABC television series ran from 1966 until 1968. The movie *Batman* (1989) featured Michael Keaton in the title role.

Beaver (Cleaver) The hapless younger son of the Cleavers in the television series "Leave It to Beaver."

Benji The shaggy mutt who became a star, appearing in *Benji* (1974), *For the Love of Benji* (1977), and *Oh Heavenly Dog* (1980).

Bert One of the muppet characters in the television series "Sesame Street." (See ERNIE and OSCAR THE GROUCH.)

Bogart (or Bogey) Humphrey Bogart, the famous actor, who starred in numerous films.

Boo-Boo Kitty Laverne's stuffed cat in the television series "Laverne and Shirley."

Bosley The man who acts as an intermediary between the elusive Charlie and his female detectives in the television series "Charlie's Angels."

Brady	The name of the family in the television series "The Brady Bunch."
Brando (Marlon)	One of the most famous American actors after World War II. Brando won Academy Awards for his performances in *On the Waterfront* (1954) and *The Godfather* (1972).
Bret Maverick	One of the brothers, played by James Garner, living in the frontier west in the television series "Maverick."
Brewster	The baseball player, played by Richard Pryor, who inherits a fortune in the movie *Brewster's Millions*.
Brubaker	The prison inspector played by Robert Redford in the movie *Brubaker*.
Buffy	The little blonde-haired girl in the television series "Buffy and Jody."
Bullet	Roy Rogers' German shepherd who debuted in the movie *Spoilers of the Plains* (1951) and later appeared on the *Roy Rogers Show*.
Burt Reynolds	Actor who has starred in a variety of movies in the 1960s, '70s, and '80s.
Butch Cassidy	The western outlaw played by Paul Newman in the 1969 movie *Butch Cassidy and the Sundance Kid*. (See SUNDANCE KID.)
Cat Ballou	The main character of the 1965 movie *Cat Ballou*.
Charlie Chaplin	One of the most famous actors in motion picture history. Chaplin is best remembered for his roles in silent films.
Cheshire Cat	The grinning cat who fades away except for his grin. Created by Lewis Carroll, the Cheshire Cat appeared in Walt Disney's animated movie *Alice in Wonderland* (1951). (See also *Cheshire Cat* in Chapter 10.)

Chewbacca (or Chewy)	The 100-year-old "Wookie" in the movie *Star Wars* (1977) and its sequels.
Chinook	The white German shepherd who costarred with Kirby Grant in a series of movies about a Mountie and his dog (1949–1954). Chinook later played White Shadow in the "Mickey Mouse Club's" Corky and White Shadow serial.
Cinderella	The fairytale heroine who marries Prince Charming in Walt Disney's animated movie *Cinderella*.
Cleo	The glum-faced basset hound who commented on the characters and events in the 1950's television show "The People's Choice."
Darth Vader	The commander of the forces of evil in the movie *Star Wars* (1977) and its sequels.
Dickenson (Angie)	An actress who has starred in both television and movie roles, including the television series "Police Woman."
Dobie Gillis	A romantically inclined teenage boy in the television series "The Many Loves of Dobie Gillis." Dobie also appeared in the movie *The Affairs of Dobie Gillis* (1953).
Doc	One of the Seven Dwarfs in Walt Disney's animated movie *Snow White and the Seven Dwarfs* (1937).
Dolly (Parton)	The country western singer and actress, who most recently appeared in her own television variety show "Dolly."
Dopey	One of the Seven Dwarfs in Walt Disney's animated movie *Snow White and the Seven Dwarfs* (1937).

Screen and Television

Dracula The vampire created by the novelist Bram Stoker, who first appeared in the 1931 movie *Dracula, The Un-Dead*.

Duchess A Parisian cat in Walt Disney's animated movie, *The Aristocats* (1970). Duchess has a romance with O'Malley, the alley cat.

Dudley (Moore) The contemporary comedian and movie star.

E.T. The extraterrestrial being in Steven Spielberg's movie *E.T.*

Elsa The lioness whose story is told in the movie *Born Free* and in a television series. Elsa's story was first told in a book by Joy Adamson.

Ernie One of the muppet characters in the television series "Sesame Street." (See BERT and OSCAR THE GROUCH.)

Ewok One of the furry, teddy bearlike creatures in the movie *The Return of the Jedi*.

Fantasia A 1940 Walt Disney feature film.

Farrah (Fawcett) The actress who first became famous in the television series "Charlie's Angels."

Festus The old deputy in the television series "Gunsmoke."

Figaro The kitten who kissed a fish in Walt Disney's animated film, *Pinocchio* (1940).

Flower The skunk in the animated feature movie *Bambi* (1942).

Fonzie	The nickname of the cool high school dropout, played by Henry Winkler, in the television series "Happy Days."
Freeway	The dog in the television series "Hart to Hart." The Harts found him on the freeway.
George Burns	A popular comedian; husband of GRACIE ALLEN.
Goofy	The not-so-bright, black hound who first appeared in Walt Disney's animated *Mickey Mouse* cartoons.
Gracie Allen	A popular comedienne; wife of GEORGE BURNS.
Grumpy	One of the Seven Dwarfs in Walt Disney's animated movie *Snow White and the Seven Dwarfs* (1937).
Happy	One of the Seven Dwarfs in Walt Disney's animated movie *Snow White and the Seven Dwarfs* (1937).
Hardy (Oliver)	The comedian who costarred with his partner, LAUREL, in numerous movies.
Harriet (Hilliard Nelson)	The wife of OZZIE in the television series "The Adventures of Ozzie and Harriet" (1952–1966).
Harrison Ford	The actor who played Hans Solo in the *Star Wars* movie series. He also played Indiana Jones in *Raiders of the Lost Ark* and its sequels.
Hawkeye	The irreverent doctor played by Alan Alda in the classic television series "M∗A∗S∗H."
Hazel (Burke)	The family maid played by Shirley Booth in the television series "Hazel."

Screen and Television

Herbie — "The Love Bug," a Volkswagen, who is the hero in several movies.

Higgins — The dog in the televison series "Petticoat Junction" (1963–1970). This was movie star BENJI's first acting role.

Hi-Ho Silver — The LONE RANGER's call to his horse in the television series "The Lone Ranger."

Huckleberry Hound — The hero of the first all-animated television series, "Huckleberry Hound," created by Hanna-Barbera Productions in 1958.

Igor — Dr. Frankenstein's assistant in a series of movies about Frankenstein's monster.

J. R. (Ewing) — The ruthless Texas oilman in the television series "Dallas."

Jerry — The famous mouse who, with his partner, the cat TOM, has appeared in numerous MGM, and later Hanna-Barbera, animated cartoons.

Joker — The sinister character of "Batman" fame played by Cesar Romero in the television series and by Jack Nicholson in the 1989 movie. (See BATMAN.)

Kingfish — George Stevens's title on the television series "Amos 'n' Andy."

Kukla, Fran & Ollie — The three puppets from the television show "Kukla, Fran, and Ollie."

Kunta Kinte — The African man captured by slave traders and shipped to America in the television mini-series *Roots* (1977).

Lady — The pretty female cocker spaniel who charmed TRAMP, a disreputable mutt, in Walt Disney Productions' *Lady and the Tramp* .

Lassie	The collie heroine of the movie *Lassie Come Home* (1943), based on a novel by Eric Knight. This Lassie, followed by many generations of descendants, starred in seven movie sequels, "The Lassie Radio Show," and the Lassie television series.
Laurel (Stan)	The slapstick comedian who costarred with his partner, HARDY, in numerous movies.
Leo	The Metro-Goldwyn-Mayer (MGM) trademark—a lion that appeared on screen in hundreds of movies.
Little Orphan Annie	The little girl created in a comic strip of the same name by Harold Gray in 1924. Little Orphan Annie has appeared in several movies, the first in 1932.
Liza (Minnelli)	The actress and singer who has appeared in numerous movies. She won an Oscar for best actress for her performance in *Cabaret*.
Lone Ranger	The masked hero of the television series "The Lone Ranger."
Luke Skywalker	The hero of the movie *Stars Wars* (1977) and its sequels.
Magnum (Thomas)	The private investigator played by Tom Selleck in the television series "Magnum, P.I."
Maynard (G. Krebs)	DOBIE GILLIS's beatnik buddy in the television series "The Many Loves of Dobie Gillis."
McCloud	The cowboy detective in the television series "McCloud."
Mia (Farrow)	An actress who has appeared in a variety of movies, including several by Woody Allen.

Mickey Mouse — The world famous star of numerous Walt Disney animated cartoons and movies, and of "The Mickey Mouse Club" television show.

Minnie Mouse — Animated cartoon star MICKEY MOUSE's female counterpart.

Miss Ellie — J. R. EWING's mother in the television series "Dallas."

Miss Kitty — The owner of Dodge City's bar in the television series "Gunsmoke."

Miss Piggy — The outrageous leading lady of television's "The Muppet Show" and of *The Muppet Movie* (1979).

Morris — The famous cat that appeared in commercials for 9-Lives Cat Food. Morris also appeared in the movie *Shamus* (1972), and in 1973 received the first Patsy Award for an animal in commercials.

Mr. T — The impressively large actor who appeared in the television series "The A-Team" and with Sylvester Stallone in one of the sequels to the movie "Rocky."

Munchkin — One of a group of little people visited by Dorothy in the cinema classic, *The Wizard of Oz*.

Oscar the Grouch — One of the muppet characters in the television series "Sesame Street." (See BERT and ERNIE.)

Old Yeller — The rugged, stray yellow-gold dog who was adopted in the movie *Old Yeller*, based on Fred Gipson's book *Old Yeller*. (See also *Old Yeller* in Chapter 10.)

Omar (Sharif) — The Middle Eastern actor who appeared in numerous movies.

007
The code number for the British spy James Bond, the hero of a series of movies based on novels by Ian Fleming.

Oscar the Grouch
One of the muppet characters in the television series "Sesame Street." (See BERT and ERNIE.)

Ozzie (Nelson)
Main character and husband of HARRIET on the television series "The Adventures of Ozzie and Harriet ."

Pebbles
Fred and Wilma Flintstone's daughter in Hanna-Barbera's animated television cartoon "The Flintstones."

Pegleg Pete
The villainous bulldog with a wooden leg who appeared with MICKEY MOUSE in the Walt Disney films, *Steamboat Willie* (1928) and *Gallopin' Gaucho* (1929).

Pepe Le Pew
The French skunk who appears in several Warner Brothers' animated cartoons.

Pete the Pup
The mongrel with a black circle around one eye and a patch over the other, who appeared in more than eighty episodes of Hal Roach's *Our Gang* comedies.

Peter Pan
The principal character in a play by J. M. Barrie about a boy who didn't want to grow up. Subsequently, he was recreated in the Walt Disney animated movie *Peter Pan*.

Pluto
Walt Disney's lovable animated hound who appears with MICKEY MOUSE in many of his cartoons.

Popeye	The sailor who derives his strength from eating spinach. Popeye appeared first in comic strips, and later in animated cartoons and movies.
Potsie	Richie Cunningham's friend in the television series "Happy Days."
Princess Leia	The heroine of the movie *Stars Wars* (1977) and its sequels.
Radar	The bespectacled corporal with E.S.P. in the television series "M*A*S*H."
Rambo	The character played by Sylvester Stallone in the movie *First Blood* and its sequels.
Rhubarb	The striped cat who played the lead role in the 1951 movie version of H. Allen Smith's *Rhubarb* (1946). Rhubarb won a Patsy Award for his performance, and then played Minerva in television's "Our Miss Brooks." In 1962, Rhubarb won another Patsy as Cat in *Breakfast at Tiffany's*.
Rin Tin Tin	The German shepherd who after his first film, *Where the North Begins* (1923), appeared in more than forty movies in nine years. His offspring, all given the same name, appeared in subsequent movies and in the television series, "The Adventures of Rin Tin Tin."
Robin	The younger half of the BATMAN and Robin combination known as "The Dynamic Duo."
Rochester (Van Jones)	Jack Benny's valet, played by Eddie Anderson.
Rockford	The private detective played by James Garner on the television series "The Rockford Files."
Rocky	The boxer played by Sylvester Stallone in the movie *Rocky* and its sequels.

Sapphire	The wife of George "Kingfish Stevens" in the television series "Amos 'n' Andy." (See KINGFISH.)
Scarlet (O'Hara)	The heroine, played by Vivian Leigh, of the classic movie *Gone With the Wind* (1939), based on the book by Margaret Mitchell.
Scraps	The white mongrel with a brown spot over one eye, who costarred with Charlie Chaplin in *A Dog's Life* (1918). Scraps went on to star in fifty more films.
Sheena	The "Queen of the Jungle" played by Irish McCalla in both the movie and the television series.
Shogun	The Japanese warrior in the television movie *Shogun*.
Sleepy	One of the Seven Dwarfs in Walt Disney's animated movie *Snow White and the Seven Dwarfs* (1937).
Sneezy	One of the Seven Dwarfs in Walt Disney's animated movie *Snow White and the Seven Dwarfs* (1937).
Snow White	The fairy tale heroine of Walt Disney's animated movie *Snow White and the Seven Dwarfs* (1937).
Solo	The puniest female pup in an African wild dog pack in Hugo van Lawick's television film *The Wild Dogs of Africa*.
Spanky	The fat little boy in the television series "The Little Rascals."
Spuds Mackenzie	The bull terrier, known as the "Party Animal," who advertises Budweiser beer in television commercials.

Strongheart The German shepherd who was the first canine hero of feature films.

Sundance Kid The western outlaw played by Robert Redford in the 1969 movie *Butch Cassidy and the Sundance Kid*. (See BUTCH CASSIDY.)

Sylvester A black-and-white cat who has appeared often with Tweety Pie, the canary, in many Warner Brothers' animated cartoons.

Sylvester Stallone The actor who has starred in the ROCKY movies and the RAMBO movies.

T. C. Thomas Magnum's friend, who pilots a helicopter in the television series "Magnum, P. I."

Tar Baby The inanimate baby who mystified all the animals in the Walt Disney movie *Song of the South* (1946); based on Joel Chandler Harris's stories.

Taylor (Elizabeth) The beautiful English-born American actress. She has appeared in numerous movies, winning Academy Awards as best actress for her performances in *Butterfield 8* (1960) and *Who's Afraid of Virginia Woolf?* (1966).

Thumper The rabbit in Walt Disney's animated movie *Bambi* (1942). (See BAMBI.)

Tigger The bouncy tiger in the animated television versions of A. A. Milne's Winnie-the-Pooh stories.

Tinkerbell The tiny fairy in the Walt Disney movie *Peter Pan*.

Toby KUNTA KINTE's name as a slave in the television mini-series *Roots* (1977).

Tom The famous cat who, with his partner, the mouse JERRY, has appeared in numerous MGM, and later Hanna-Barbera animated cartoons.

Tonto | The LONE RANGER's Indian companion in both the movie and the television series about "The Lone Ranger."

Tootsie | The man-turned-woman, played by Dustin Hoffman in the movie *Tootsie*.

Toto | Dorothy's dog in the movie *The Wizard of Oz* (1939).

Tramp | The stray dog who fell in love with LADY, the pretty cocker spaniel, in Walt Disney Productions' animated feature *Lady and the Tramp*.

Trapper | HAWKEYE's buddy in the television series "M∗A∗S∗H."

Wally (Cleaver) | BEAVER's older brother in the television series "Leave It to Beaver."

Wile E. Coyote | The hapless pursuer of Road Runner in a series of animated films.

Yoda | LUKE SKYWALKER's mentor who trains Luke to become a Jedi in the movies *The Empire Strikes Back* and *Return of the Jedi*.

Yogi (Bear) | The hero of the animated television cartoon "Yogi Bear," who lives in Jellystone National Park.

Yukon King | The husky who aided Sergeant Preston of the Northwest Mounted Police in his television show, "Sergeant Preston of the Yukon."

Zeus | One of the two Doberman pinschers owned by Robbin Masters on the television series "Magnum P.I." (See APOLLO.)

CHAPTER 12
Locations and Places

You don't know what a country we have got till you start prowling around it. Personally, I like the small places and sparsely populated states.

Will Rogers

If you're caught without a map or atlas, herein you'll find that little spot you've been looking for. Or, pick your favorite place as your pet's name. Be creative; be original; be anything or anywhere, but don't let your pet be without a name.

Locations and Places

Acapulco (Mexico)

Africa

Amazon (A river in South America.)

Asia

Aspen (Colorado)

Austin (Texas)

Bali

Baltic

Bangkok (Thailand)

Bangladesh

Barbados

Bayou (A marshy creek.)

Beijing (China)

Belgium

Bogotá (Colombia)

Broadway (The "Great White Way" in New York City.)

Burma

Cairo (Eygpt)

Camelot (The legendary capital of Arthur's kingdom.)

Cancun (Mexico)

Chelsea (A district in London and in New York City.)

China

Colorado (Rado)

Congo

Cozumel (Mexico)

D. C. (Washington, District of Columbia)

Dallas (Texas)

Delaware (Dele)

Denmark

Dixie (A traditional name for the South.)

Egypt

El Dorado (The legendary City of Gold of the Spanish explorers.)

Fiji

France

Freeway (A limited-access highway.)

Greece

Hawaii

Hilton (A hotel chain.)

Holland (The Netherlands)

Hyatt (A hotel chain.)

India

Ixtapa (Mexico)

Jamaica

Junk Yard Cat

Junk Yard Dog

Katamandu (Nepal)

Kaunai

K. C. (Kansas City, Kansas and Missouri)

Kenya

Keys (A chain of islands off the southern tip of Florida.)

L. A.

Loch Ness (Scotland)

Madrid (Spain)

Manzanillo (Mexico)

Marriot (A hotel chain.)

Mazatlán (Mexico)

Maui

Memphis (Tennessee)

Montana

Nassau

Nepal

Nile (A river in East Africa.)

Oahu

Locations and Places

Oslo (Norway)

Peking (China)

Persia

Phoenix (Arizona)

P.V. (Puerto Vallarta, Mexico)

Randolph

Reykjavik (Iceland)

Rio (Rio de Janeiro, Brazil)

Ritz (A luxury hotel.)

Siam

Sidney (Australia)

Spain

Tahiti

Taipei

Tara (A village in Ireland.)

Texas (Tex)

Tibet

Tripoli (Libya)

Turkey

Utah

Vegas (Las Vegas, Nevada)

Venice (Italy)

Virginia

"Fraidy"

CHAPTER 13

Unusual Names and Nicknames

. . . people select names for some private reason or for no reason at all—except to arouse a visitor's curiosity, so that he will exclaim, 'Why in the world do you call your dog that?' The cryptic name their dogs October, Bennet's Aunt, Three Fifteen, Doc Knows, Tuesday, Home Fried, Opus 38, Ask Leslie, and Thanks for the Home Run, Emil. I make it a point simply to pat these unfortunate dogs on the head, ask no questions of their owners, and go about my business.

James Thurber
from "How to Name a Dog"

One of my clients once told me she had considered renaming her dog after she had to stand in her front yard at midnight calling "Woogie, here Woogie."

But if you're not likely to be concerned with what other people think, be as outrageous as your imagination will allow.

Unusual Names and Nicknames

A. J.	Blowout	Buffer	Chance
Ace	Blue	Buffin	Chancy
Alfie	Bo	Buffy	Chap
Allie	Bobbi	Bullet	Chapin
Alpha	Bobby	Bun Bun	Chappy
Apache	Bobo	Buster	Chaps
April	Bomber	Butch	Charlette
Aztec	Boo	Butterfingers	Charley
B. B.	Boo Boo	Button(s)	Charli
B. J.	Boogie	Buzz	Charlie
Bad Debt	Booh	Ca Cee	Charmin
Bandi	Boomer	Cai	Cheebe
Bark-ley	Boots	Cali	Cheers
Bartholo-mew	Bootsie	Calley	Chelsea
Beau Beau	Bowser	Callie	Chelsey
Beaux	Bozo	Cally	Chelsia
Bebe	Bravo	Candi	Chelsie
Bee	Briana	Caprice	Cheri
Belle	Bubah	Captain Happy	Chickie
Beta	Bubba	Career Girl	Chicle
Big Foot	Buck	Cat Astrophe	Chief
Bingo	Buckshot	Catsanova	Chilla
Binky	Bud	Cee Gee	Chimpy
Blaze	Buddy	Chainsaw	Chris

Chrisitiana	Cowboy	Dy	Goofie Bear
Chrissy	Crash	Elkie	Grammar
Christabel	Cricket	Esti	H. T.
Christmas	Critter	Eulika	Hailey
Chu Chu	Crockett Cat	Ewoke	Hazard
Chuckles	Crystal	Exxene	Hef
Chump	Cuki	Fella	Helen Dalmation
Chuska	D. D.	Fifi	Hi Pockets
Cici	Daffy	Fila	Holly Hobbles
Cinder	Dagney	Flakes	Hooter
Cio Cio Sam	Dahli	Flaps	Inca
Cisco	Dawg	Flower	J. D.
Clazy	Dax	Fluffer	J. J.
Co Co	Deli	Fluffles	Jammer
Coco	Dexter	Fragment	Jasmine
Coco Bear	Dobie	Fraidy	Jenn-i-purr
Codie	Donation	Friday	Jillsy
Cody	Doxy	Fusby	Jingles
Collie	Dude	Ged	Jinx
Comanche	Dudlee	Ghillie	Jip
Cooler	Duffy	Gi Gi	Jo Jo
Corky	Duster	Gink	Joker
Cotton	Dusty	Gizmo	Jossie
Cottontail	Dutch	Goober	Jr.

Unusual Names and Nicknames

Jukie	Kitti	Mac Duff	Missy
Jumbo	Kitty Boy	Mackie	Misty
Justa Cat	Kitty Carlyle	Maddie	Mitch
Justa Dog	Kitty Q	Mail	Mitzi
K. C.	Knuckles	Majic	Mitzie
K. D.	Kobi	Mama Trouble	Mitzu
K. J.	Kodak	Mary Dog	Mixture
Kadee	Kristil	Maverick	Mo
Kali	Kuchen	Maxi	Moe
Kally	Kyrie	Mc Gruffen	Moffie
Kat	Lace	Meetsie	Mofford
Kater	Lacey	Meow	Mo Jo
Keesha	Lady Gal	Mercy	Molley
Keeta	Lady Lin	Merry	Moma
Kelli	Lexie	Christmas	Momma Dog
Key Key	Lia	Mew	(Cat)
Keys	Li'l Guy	Mew Mew	Moo Moo
Kiki	Li'l Honeysuckle	Middie	Mopsy
Kinki	Little B	Miffy	Mortikie
Kit Kat	Little Bit	Mimi	Morty
Kitsy	Little Girl	Mimie	Moss
Kitt	Little Kitty	Minni	Mr. Cuddles
Kittens	Lobo	Minnie	Mr. Kitty
Kitter	Lou Lou	Miss Kitty	Mr. Stubbs

Mrs. T	(Pari)	Princess Daisy	Raven
Ms. Muffet	Peace	Princess Josette	Razz
Muff	Pee Dee	Princess Tiffany	Razzy
Muffer	Pennie	Priss	Reggie
Muffett	Penny	Prissy	Remington
Muffie	Peppy	Pudder	Ringo
Muffy	Petunia	Puffy	Rinky Dink
Muggs	Phideaux	Punky	Rip
Mutzie	Pinky	Pup	Rockey
Navajo	Pitney	Pupdog	Rodeo
New Kitty	Podnah	Pupper	Rolf
Nicky	Pojoo	Puppy	Rollie
Nic Nac	Poli	Pups	Romer
Niki	Ponch	Pupus	Roo
Nikke	Poo Bee Bear	Purr Son	Rosco
Odd Ball	Pooch	Purrbert	Roscoe
Okie	Poochie	Puss Cat	Rose
Ombre	Poochkie	Pussy	Rosebud
P. B.	Pooky	R. B.	Rosie
P. C.	Pooper	Rags	Roxy
P. C. Jr.	Poops	Rainbow	Ruffles
P. J.	Poppy	Rascal	Samba (o)
Pandy	Potsi	Rat	Sami
Paraphernalia	Pozzo	Ratus	Sarg

Unusual Names and Nicknames

Sashi	Sissie	Sooka	Supplies
Sassy	Sissy	Sparky	Suzie Queen
Sassy San	Sister	Special	T. C.
Saturday	Skeeter	Spike	T. J.
Saucer	Skinner	Spiker	Taffi
Sawdust	Skipper	Spikey	Tai
Scamp	Skippy	Splash	Tally
Schwatz	Skitty	Spooner	Tashi
Scottie	Skunky	Sport	Tasi
Shammy	Skwiggles	Spring	Taski
Sheba	Slick	Spunky	Tatters
Sheeba	Smitty	Squish	Tattoo
Shimmy	Snapper de Aire	Star	Tawnya
Shinola	Snert	Stardust	Tennie
Shoebutton	Snoobie	Starr	Tex
Shorty Bob	Snooker	Stash	Thunder
Shotie	Snooky	Static	Tic Tac
Shu Shu	Snoops	Stormy	Tick Tock
Si	Snowball	Strubie	Ticker
Siah	Snow Bear	Sunday	Tidbit
Silver Bell	Snubbs	Sunnie	Tiffy
Sioux	Sonny	Sunny	Tiko
Sir Chadwick	Soo	Sunny Cat	Tinker
Sir Woody	Soo Shi	Sunspot	Tippy

Tipsy	Trapper	Wagley	Willow
Tobe	Trixie	Waterford	Winkie
Tobi	Trooper	Weebles	Wisky Blue
Tobia	Trouffels	Wetta	Wizard
Toodles	Tuffy	Whacker	Woogy
Toot	Turbo	Whiz Bang	YoYo
Toot Toot	Tusche	Whiz O	Zac
Tootie	Twinkle Toes	Wicket	Zee
Tootsie	Twit	Wifferdill	Zero
Topper	Velcro	Wildfire	Zip

"Splash"

CHAPTER 14

Cartoon Characters

Peanuts characters © copyright 1950, 1952, 1958 by United Features Syndicate.

Charles Schultz
from *You Don't Look 35, Charlie Brown*

Your pet may be the perfect Daffy Duck or Roadrunner—guaranteed to make you laugh. But plan ahead! When he or she is testing your patience, a stern "Jughead, I told you to behave!" may change your stern countenance into a smiling face.

Cartoon Characters

Albert	A main character in "POGO."
Alley Oop	Title character.
Alvin	A character in "The CHIPMUNKS."
Al Capp	Cartoonist; creator of "LIL' ABNER."
Andy Capp	Title character.
Animal Crackers	Title character.
Annie (Little Orphan)	Title character.
Archie	Title character.
B. C.	Title character.
Bam Bam	A character in "The FLINTSTONES."
Barney Rubble	A character in "The FLINTSTONES."
Beatle Bailey	Title character.
Beauregard Bugleboy	A character in "POGO."
Betty	A character in "The FLINTSTONES."
Betty Boop	Title character.
Blondie	Title character.

Bonzo	Title character.
Brainey	A character in "The SMURFS."
Brutus	A villain in "POPEYE."
Bugs Bunny	Title character.
Bumstead	DAGWOOD's and BLONDIE's family name.
Buster Brown	Title character.
Calvin	Title character in "Calvin and HOBBES."
Cap Stubbs	Title character.
Caspar	Title character: "Caspar the Friendly Ghost."
Charlie Brown	Costar of comic strip and television series "PEANUTS."
Chip	Title character in "Chip and DALE."
Chipmunk(s)	Title character(s).
Daffy Duck	Title character.
Dagwood	BLONDIE's husband.
Daisy	DONALD DUCK's girlfriend.
Daisy Mae	LIL' ABNER's girlfriend.

Dale	Title character in "CHIP and Dale."
Dennis the Menace	Title character.
Dick Tracy	Title character.
Dinny	ALLEY OOP's pet dinosaur.
Donald Duck	Title character; also MICKEY MOUSE's friend.
Doonesbury	Title of strip.
Elmer Fudd	A character in "DAFFY DUCK."
Elwood	Title character.
Felix the Cat	Title character.
Flintstone(s)	Title character(s).
Fred Basset	Title character.
Fritz	A character in "The KATZENJAMMER KIDS."
Fritz the Cat	Title character.
Garfield	Title character.
Gertie	Title character in "Gertie, the Trained Dinosaur."
Goofy	A character in "MICKEY MOUSE."

Gordo	Title character.
Grammy	Title character.
Gumby	Title character in "Gumby and POKEY."
Gummi Bear	Title character.
Hagar the Horrible	Title character.
Hans	A character in "The KATZENJAMMER KIDS."
Hazel	Title character.
Heathcliff	Title character.
Heckle and Jeckle	Title character.
Henry	Title character.
Hobbes	Title character in "CALVIN and Hobbes."
Huckleberry Hound	Title character.
Ignatz Mouse	Title character.
Jeff	Title character in "MUTT and Jeff."
Jerry	Title character in "TOM and Jerry."
Jiggs	A character in the cartoon strip "Bringing Up Father."

Cartoon Characters

Joe Cool	SNOOPY's alter ego in "PEANUTS."
Jughead	A character in "ARCHIE."
Katzenjammer Kids	Title character(s).
Krazy Kat	Title character.
Li'l Abner	Title character.
Linus	A character in comic strip and television series "PEANUTS."
Little Abner	Title character.
Little Lulu	Title character.
Luann	Title character.
Lucy	A character in "PEANUTS."
Maggie	A character in "Bringing Up Father."
Margaret	A character in "DENNIS THE MENACE."
Marmaduke	Title character.
Maw	A character in "SNUFFY SMITH."
Mickey Mouse	Title character.
Mighty Mouse	Title character.

Minnie Mouse	MICKEY MOUSE's girlfriend.
Moon Mullins	Title character.
Mr. Boffo	Title character.
Mr. Magoo	Title character.
Mutt	Title character in "Mutt and JEFF."
Nancy	Title character.
Napoleon	Title character.
Nermal	Cat in "GARFIELD" comics.
Nervy Nat	Title character.
Nudnik	Title character.
Odie	GARFIELD's canine friend.
Offisa Bull Pupp	A character in "KRAZY KAT."
Okefenokee	The setting (a swamp) in the series "POGO."
Olive Oil	POPEYE's girlfriend.
Opus	The penguin in the comic strip series "Bloom County."
Peanuts	Title of comic strip and television series.

Cartoon Characters

Pebbles	A character in the comic strip and television series "The FLINTSTONES."
Pepe Le Pew	A character in "BUGS BUNNY and Friends."
Peppermint Patty	A character in the comic strip and television series "PEANUTS."
Petunia Pig	A character in "PORKY PIG."
Phineas T. Bridgeport	A character in "POGO."
Pig-Pen	A character in the comic strip and television series "PEANUTS."
Pink Panther	Title character.
Pluto	MICKEY MOUSE's dog.
Pogo	Title character.
Pokey	Title character in "GUMBY and Pokey."
Popeye	Title character.
Porky Pig	Title character.
Prince Valiant	Title character.
Road Runner	Title character.
Rose	Title character in "Rose is Rose."
Ruff	A character in "DENNIS THE MENACE."

Sally	A character in the comic strip and television series "PEANUTS."
Schroeder	A character in the comic strip and television series "PEANUTS."
Scooby Doo	Title character.
Simon	Title character: "The CHIPMUNKS."
Simple J. Malarkey	A character in "POGO."
Smurf	Title character.
Smurfette	A character in "The SMURFS."
Snoopy	Title character in the comic strip and television series "PEANUTS."
Snuffy Smith	Title character.
Solomon	Title character.
Speedy Gonzales	Title character.
Spike	A character in "TOM and JERRY."
Steve Canyon	Title character.
Sylvester	Title character.
Tintin	Title character.
Tippie	Title character in a comic strip no longer in print.

Cartoon Characters

Tom — Title character in "Tom and JERRY."

Trudy — Title character.

Tweetie Pie — A character in the comic strip and animated cartoon "SYLVESTER the Cat."

Veronica — A character in "ARCHIE."

Wile E. Coyote — A character in the comic strip and animated cartoon "The ROAD RUNNER."

Wiley Catt — A character in "POGO."

Wilma — A character in the comic strip and television series "The FLINTSTONES."

Wimpie — A character in the comic strip and animated cartoon "POPEYE."

Winnie-the-Pooh — Title character.

Woodstock — A character in the comic strip and television series "PEANUTS."

Yogi — Title character in "Yogi the Bear."

Zero — A character in "BEATLE BAILEY."

Ziggy — Title character.

"Primadonna"

CHAPTER 15

Just for Fun

But I tell you, a cat needs a name that's particular,
A name that's peculiar, and more dignified,
Else how can he keep up his tail perpendicular,
Or spread out his whiskers, or cherish his pride?

T. S. Eliot
from *Old Possum's Book of Practical Cats* (1939)

A school mascot or the name of a singer may become your new pet's name. Use this short chapter to give you some ideas; there are only a few names suggested here to get you started on your own list.

Just for Fun

Aggie	Danny Boy	Mel Tilles	Rock
Ballerina	Disco	Miss Emily	Rocket(s)
Banjo	Doc	Moe Bandy	Sailor
Banker	Elvis	Mrs. Robinson	Sergeant Pepper
Bartender	Gig 'em	Nittany Lion	Shasta
Bevo	Harry Chapin	Pavarotti	Sooner
Bill Bailey	Hoosier	Pilot	Tango
Bob Dylan	Horned Toad	Primadonna	Tom Dooley
Boogie	Julio Iglesias	Prof	Trucker
Cha Cha	Lawyer	Razorback	Uga
Charger	Louis Armstrong	Red Raider	Waylon
Chet Atkins	Madonna	Reville	Jennings
D. J.	Manager	Ringo Starr	Willie Nelson

"Slam Dunk"

CHAPTER 16
Sports

The game ain't over till it's over.

Yogi (Lawrence Peter) Berra

Throughout the past century, sports has played a big part in our lives. Whether you are an avid sports buff or a part-time fan keeping up with your favorite team, consider some of these entries in your selection of your pet's name.

Sports

A. J. Foyt	A famous race car driver; four-time Indy 500 winner.
Ace	In tennis, an unreturnable serve.
Adidas	A brand of athletic wear.
Al Worthington	Baseball: A pitcher for the Giants in the fifties and the Twins and the White Sox in the sixties.
Amy Alcott	Golf: 1980 U.S. Women's Open Champion.
Arnold Palmer	Golf: Winner of four Masters Tournaments, one U.S. Open, and two British Open Tournaments.
Babe Ruth	Baseball: One of the most famous all-time athletes, Ruth hit 60 home runs in 1927 while playing for the New York Yankees.
Balk	In baseball, an incomplete or misleading motion.
Bart Starr	Football: Hall of Famer; active 1965 to 1973; associated mainly with the Chicago Bears.
Batter	In baseball, the player attempting to hit the ball.
Bear Bryant	Football: Coach at Texas A & M University in the fifties and at the University of Alabama in the sixties, seventies, and eighties.
Ben Hogan	Golf: Winner of four U.S. Opens. In 1953, he won the Masters, the U.S. Open, and the British Open.
Billy Jean King	Tennis: Winner of several Indoor, U.S. Open, and Wimbledon titles (among others) during the 1960s and 1970s.

Birdie — In Golf, a score of one under PAR.

Bo Jackson — Football: 1985 Heisman Memorial Trophy winner (Auburn University).

Bob Cousy — Basketball: A Boston Celtics standout, Cousy scored 50 points in a 1953 playoff game—a record at the time.

Bobby Hull — Ice Hockey: Player, elected to the Hall of Fame, having spent the most productive years with the Chicago Black Hawks.

Bobby Mitchell — Football: First black player to be a member of the Washington Redskins; he was later elected to the Hall of Fame.

Bogey — In golf, a score of one over PAR.

Boog Powell — Baseball: Outfielder for the Baltimore Orioles in the sixties and seventies; best known for his appearance on Miller Lite beer commercials.

Boxer — In boxing, one who fights with his fists.

Bunker — In golf, a sand TRAP.

Carl Lewis — Track and Field: World record holder in the 100-Meter Dash and the 200-Meter Dash (1984 Summer Olympic Games).

Casey Stengel — Baseball: Former manager of the New York Yankees; led his team to ten American League pennant titles from 1949 to 1980.

Cassius Clay — See MUHAMMAD ALI.

Catcher — In baseball, the player who receives the pitches from the PITCHER.

Sports

Center	In football, the player who hands the ball to the QUARTERBACK.
Charley Taylor	Football: A receiver for the Washington Redskins who caught a record 649 passes from 1964 to 1977.
Chris Evert	Tennis: Winner of several indoor, U.S. Open, and Wimbledon titles (among others) during the 1970s and 1980s.
Clipping	In football, an illegal maneuver in which the opposing player is BLOCKED from behind.
Dan Marino	Football: First all-time leading passer in the NFL.
Dick Butkus	Football: Hall of Famer; active 1965 to 1973; associated mainly with Chicago Bears.
Dizzy Dean	Baseball: Winner of National League's Most Valuable Player Award, 1934.
Doug Flutie	Football: Heisman Memorial Trophy winner (Boston College).
Dribble	In basketball, bouncing the ball on the floor.
Driver	In golf, the club normally used on the tee box for attaining distance.
Eagle	In golf, a score of two under PAR.
Earl Campbell	Football: 1977 Heisman Memorial Trophy winner (University of Texas).
Evonne Goolagong	Tennis: Winner at Wimbledon in 1971 and 1980.
Extra Point	In football, scoring a point after a TOUCHDOWN.

Fastball	In baseball, a PITCH thrown at a high rate of speed.
Featherweight	In boxing, a BOXER weighing between 118 and 127 pounds.
Florence Griffith	Track and Field: 1988 Olympic gold medalist.
Floyd Patterson	Boxing: World HEAVYWEIGHT champion, 1956 to 1959, 1960 to 1962.
Fly Ball	In baseball, a pitch which is hit high into the air.
Flyweight	In boxing, a BOXER in the lightest weight class (weighing 112 pounds or less).
Frisbee	A brand of toy that resembles a "flying saucer."
Fullback	In football, a player in the BACKFIELD.
Fumble	In football, the act of an offensive ball carrier dropping the ball.
George Foreman	Boxing: World HEAVYWEIGHT champion, 1970 to 1973.
Goal	In ice hockey, the area behind the net through which players try to advance a PUCK. In basketball, the HOOP into which players throw a ball.
Goalie	In ice hockey, the player who defends the GOAL.
Grounder	In baseball, a ball hit on the ground by the BATTER.
Gutter	In bowling, the area on either side of the lane.
Halfback	In football, a player in the BACKFIELD.

Hand-off	In football, one offensive player giving the ball to another offensive player.
Hank Aaron	Baseball: Hall of Famer and holder of the following records: Home runs (1st), Runs scored (2nd), and Hits (3rd).
Hazard	An obstacle on a golf course.
Heavyweight	In boxing, the class of BOXERS in the heaviest weight class, weighing over 175 pounds.
Hershel Walker	Football: 1982 Heisman Memorial Trophy winner (University of Georgia).
Hit-and-Run	In baseball, a play in which the runner progresses to the next base simultaneously with the BATTER hitting the PITCH.
Hollis Stacy	Golf: 1977 and 1978 U.S. Women's Open champion.
Home Run	In baseball, a play in which the ball hit by the BATTER allows him to proceed around all three bases safely to home plate.
Homer	See HOME RUN.
Hoop	In basketball, the GOAL.
Interception	In football, a play in which a defensive player catches a pass in the air.
Jack Dempsey	Boxing: World HEAVYWEIGHT champion, 1919 to 1926.
Jack Nicklaus	Golf: Winner of the following tournaments: six Masters, four U.S. Opens, five PGA's, and three British Opens.

Jackie Joyner-Kersee	Track and Field: 1988 Olympic gold medalist.
Jan Stephenson	Golf: 1983 U.S. Women's Open champion.
Jane Geddes	Golf: 1986 U.S. Women's Open champion.
Janet Alex	Golf: 1982 U.S. Women's Open champion.
Jesse Owens	Track and Field: Winner of four Olympic gold medals in 1936.
Jim Brown	Football: Professional football Hall of Famer; Cleveland Browns, 1957 to 1965.
Jim Thorpe	Pentathlon and Decathlon: 1912 Olympics in Stockholm, Sweden.
Joe DiMaggio	Baseball: Former New York Yankees outfielder; hit safely in 50 consecutive baseball games.
Joe Frazier	Boxing: World HEAVYWEIGHT champion, 1970 to 1973.
Joe Louis	Boxing: World HEAVYWEIGHT champion from 1937 to 1950.
Joe Montana	Football: Second all-time leading passer in the NFL.
Joe Namath	Football: The New York Jets QUARTERBACK and Hall of Famer (1985); led his team to a 16–7 victory over the Baltimore Colts in the 1968 football season Super Bowl.
Julius Irving	Basketball: Third lifetime NBA leading scorer (30,026 points through 1988 season).

Jump Shot	In basketball, a play in which the ball is propelled toward the GOAL while the player is airborne.
Kareem Abdul-Jabbar	Basketball: Lew Alcindor; Individual NBA scoring champion 1960 to 1972; Milwaukee Bucs.
Kathy Baker	Golf: 1985 U.S. Women's Open champion.
Kickoff	In football, putting the ball into play by kicking it to the opposing team from a stationary position on the ground.
Knuckleball	In baseball, a pitch thrown by gripping the ball with the knuckles of two or three fingers.
KO (Knockout)	In boxing, defeating an opponent by causing him to fall onto the canvas and remain there for a count of ten.
Larry Bird	Basketball: High-scoring forward of the Boston Celtics; winner of the NBA Most Valuable Player Award, 1984.
Laura Davies	Golf: 1987 U.S. Women's Open champion.
Layup	In basketball, a shot made by playing the ball off the backboard from close to the basket, usually after driving in.
Lightweight	In boxing, a BOXER weighing between 127 and 135 pounds.
Liselott Neuman	Golf: 1988 U.S. Women's Open champion.
Lob	In basketball, volleyball, and tennis, a shot that attains greater height than normal.

Lou Gehrig	Baseball: Hall of Famer; active from 1923 to 1939; holder of 10th Highest Runs Scored record.
Magic Johnson	Basketball: Winner of the NBA Most Valuable Player Award, 1987; member of the Los Angeles Lakers.
Martina Navratilova	Tennis: Winner of several indoor, U.S. Open and Wimbledon titles during the late 1970s and 1980s.
Maury Wills	Baseball: Los Angeles Dodgers' shortstop who set a record in 1962 by stealing 104 bases.
Michael Jordan	Basketball: NBA Individual Scoring champion 1986 to 1988 (Chicago Bulls).
Michael Spinks	Boxing: World HEAVYWEIGHT champion, 1985 to 1986.
Mickey Mantle	Baseball: New York Yankees outfielder who led the American League in home runs four seasons. During his career with the Yankees from 1952 to 1968, his team won 11 pennants and seven World Championships.
Middleweight	In boxing, a BOXER weighing between 148 and 160 pounds.
Mike Tyson	Boxing: World HEAVYWEIGHT champion 1987 to 1989.
Muhammed Ali	Boxing: World HEAVYWEIGHT champion, 1964 to 1967; 1974 to 1978; and 1978 to 1979.
Net	In tennis and volleyball, the barrier of meshwork cord that divides the playing field; also, in basketball, the cord under the rim on the backboard.
Nike	A brand of sportswear/shoes.

Nolan Ryan	Baseball: Record holder for most number of lifetime strikeouts by a pitcher (broke 5,000 mark in 1989).
O.B.	"Out of bounds": In football and certain other games, the term applies to a ball out of play.
O. J. Simpson	Football: Winner of the 1968 Heisman Memorial Trophy (USC); The first choice at the 1969 pro football draft in which he was paid $250,000 over four years, the most paid for a running back. He later became a sports commentator for ABC and NBC. *Was arrested for wife's murder (1994*
Pancho Gonzales	Tennis: Player who dominated the pro tour from 1953 to 1962.
Par	In golf, the score standard for each of the holes on a golf course.
Pat Bradley	Golf: 1981 U.S. Women's Open champion.
Penalty	A loss of advantage enforced on a player or team for infraction of a rule.
Pete Rose	Baseball: Leader in total number of lifetime hits (4,256); played mostly with the Cincinnati Reds; suspended in 1989 for betting on baseball.
Pistol Pete	Basketball: Pete Maravich, holder of two college top Single-Game Scoring records: 1969 (66 points); 1970 (69 points); also leading Individual NBA scorer in 1976 to 1977 (2,273 points).
Pitch	In baseball, the term used for the ball when it is thrown by the PITCHER to the BATTER.
Pitcher	In baseball, one who throws the ball to the BATTER.
Pitchout	In baseball, a PITCH deliberately thrown high and outside making it easy for the CATCHER to retrieve.

Popup	In baseball, a ball hit high into the air by the BATTER.
Puck	In ice hockey, the hard rubber disc used in play instead of a ball.
Punt	In football, a kick in which the ball is kicked when dropped from the hands before it touches the ground.
Putter	In golf, the club used to hit the ball into the cup on the green.
Quarterback	In football, the player who receives the ball from the CENTER, calls the signals, and directs the offensive plays of the team.
Randy Matson	Track and field: The Texas A & M shotputter who broke the world record in 1967; he won an Olympic gold medal the following year.
Rebound	In basketball, the act of retrieving and recovering the ball after a missed shot.
Recovery	In football, the act of regaining possession of the ball after a fumble.
Red Auerbach	Basketball: Former coach of the Boston Celtics.
Red Grange	Football: Illinois University player in the 1920s; he was known as "The Galloping Ghost."
Reebok	A brand of sportswear/shoes.
Referee (Ref)	The official who enforces the rules in sports games.
Reggie Jackson	Baseball: American League Home Run champion 1973, 1975, and 1980.
Rocky Marciano	Boxing: World HEAVYWEIGHT champion, 1952 to 1956.

Sports

Roger Maris	Baseball: Former New York Yankees player; hit more home runs in one season than any other player in history (61 in 1961).
Rugby	A British game which has similarities to American football, basketball, soccer, and hockey.
Runner	In baseball, the player who attempts to round the bases; also a person who jogs or runs.
Sacrifice	In baseball, a play in which the BATTER is out but a RUNNER advances to another base.
Safety	In football, the grounding of the ball by the offensive team behind its own goal line; a defensive player farthest from the line of SCRIMMAGE.
Sandy Koufax	Baseball: Los Angeles Dodgers' pitcher who won the Cy Young Award in 1963, 1965, and 1966.
Scrimmage	A team's practice session.
Server	In tennis, volleyball and certain other games, the player who brings the ball into play.
Shotgun	A gun that fires multiple pellets through a smooth bore.
Skeet	A sport in which clay targets are thrown into the air and fired at from eight different stations.
Sky Hook	In basketball, a hook shot which attains more than usual height.
Slam Dunk	In basketball, the maneuver in which a player forces the ball into the net from above the rim.

Slingshot	A Y-shaped instrument with elastic bands attached; used for propelling objects.
Snap	In football, the handing of the ball to the QUARTERBACK through the legs of the CENTER.
Sonny Liston	Boxing: World HEAVYWEIGHT champion 1962 to 1964.
Spar	In boxing, going through the motions of boxing.
Spare	In bowling, knocking down all ten pins with two successive rolls of the ball.
Sparky Anderson	Baseball: Manager of the Cinncinati Reds until 1979 at which time he became manager of the Detroit Tigers.
Speedo	Brand of swimwear.
Spoon	Giving the ball an upward movement in certain games.
Stan Musial	Baseball: Player for the St. Louis Cardinals in the fifties and sixties; a Hall of Famer, Musial held National League records for having played more games (3,026) than any other National Leaguer; he also held league records for most runs batted in, most at bats, most runs scored, and most base hits.
Steffi Graff	Tennis: Winner of several U.S. Open, Indoor and Wimbledon titles during the 1980s.
Strike	In baseball, a PITCH that the BATTER misses; also, a PITCH that crosses without the BATTER making any attempt to swing.

Swish	In basketball, a shot that passses through the rim without touching it.
T. D. (Touchdown)	See TOUCHDOWN.
T.K.O.	Boxing: Technical knock out. This occurs when a match is ended because one of the boxers is unable to continue fighting, but has not been knocked down and counted out by the referee.
Tackle	In football, stopping another player by seizing him and bringing him to the ground; the players positioned between the guard and the end.
Ted Williams	Baseball: National Hall of Famer; six time American League Batting champion from 1939 to 1960.
Tim Brown	Football: 1987 Heisman Memorial Trophy winner.
Tony Dorsett	Football: 1976 Heisman Memorial Trophy winner.
Touchback	In football, touching the ball to the ground behind one's own goal line, the ball having been impelled over the goal line by an opponent.
Touchdown	In football, scoring six points.
Trap	In golf, an area filled with sand to serve as a HAZARD.
Ty Cobb	Baseball: A Detroit Tigers' player in the early 1900s who had a lifetime batting average of .367 and 4,191 base hits. He was the first member of the National Baseball Hall of Fame.
Umpire (Ump)	A person designated to rule on various plays, especially in baseball.

Vince Lombardi	Football. Hall of Famer; coach of the Green Bay Packers and Washington Redskins from 1959 to 1970.
Volley	In tennis and volleyball, a series of successive returns of the ball from one side to the other.
Wedge	In golf, a club with the head positioned at a large angle to allow for loft when the ball is hit.
Welterweight	In boxing, a BOXER who weighs between 136 and 147 pounds.
Whitey Ford	Baseball: New York Yankees pitcher in the fifties and sixties; holder of the following lifetime World Series records: Most Victories (pitcher), Most Innings Pitched, Most Consecutive Scoreless Innings, and Most Strikeouts by Pitcher.
Willie Mays	Baseball: San Francisco Giants and New York Mets outfielder who had a career batting average of .302. His lifetime total of 660 homers was topped only by BABE RUTH and HANK AARON; Hall of Famer.
Wilson	Brand of sports equipment.
Wilt Chamberlain	Basketball: Star of the Philadelphia Warriors and the Los Angeles Lakers, scoring a record 100 points in one game. He averaged 50.4 points per game during the 1961 to 1962 season.
Wimbledon	In tennis, the home of the World Championships since 1908.
Yogi Berra	Baseball: Hall of Famer; active 1946 to 1965. Holder of record number of hits (71) in World Series (lifetime).

"Edsel"

CHAPTER 17
Transportation

. . . He gives you a wave of his long brown tail
Which says: "I'll see you again!"
You'll meet without fail on the Midnight Mail
The Cat of the Railway Train.

T. S. Eliot
from *Old Possum's Book of Practical Cats* (1939)

Flight 524 now boarding at Gate 3.

If you need assistance, please ask your flight attendant for suggestions.

Should you be traveling by car, watch for "Alfa Romeo" and "Ferrari"; they're fast and sometimes difficult to see.

Guarantee your reservation by selecting one of the choices in this chapter. (Cancellations must be made prior to 6 P.M. the day of your pet's arrival.)

Accord	An automobile made by Honda.
Acura	A luxury automobile made by Honda.
Alfa Romeo	An Italian sports car.
Bentley	A luxury automobile made by ROLLS ROYCE.
Blazer	A recreational vehicle made by Chevrolet.
BMW	A German-made luxury automobile.
Boeing	An aircraft manufacturer.
Boxcar	A fully enclosed freight car.
Bronco	A recreational vehicle made by FORD.
Bugatti	An Italian sports car.
Buggy	A light, horse-drawn carriage.
Buick	An automobile made by General Motors.
Bus	A large passenger vehicle; also sometimes applied to an old car.
Cadillac	A luxury automobile made by General Motors.
Celica	A sports car made by TOYOTA.
Chevy	Chevrolet: an automobile made by General Motors.

Chrysler	An American automobile/manufacturer.
Corvette	A sports car made by Chevrolet. (See CHEVY.)
DeLorean	An automobile designed and manufactured by John DeLorean in the early 1980s in Belfast, Northern Ireland.
DeSoto	An automobile formerly made by CHRYLSER.
Dodge	An automobile made by CHRYSLER.
Edsel	An automobile formerly made by FORD.
Ferrari	An Italian sports car.
Ford	An American automobile/manufacturer.
Harley	An American-made motorcycle manufactured by Harley-Davidson, Inc
Helicopter (Chopper)	An aircraft powered by a rotor.
Honda	A Japanese automobile/manufacturer.
Jaguar	A British luxury automobile.
Jeep	An American "general purpose vehicle."
Jet	A type of aircraft engine that propels an aircraft forward by expelling exhaust gases rearward.
Lincoln	American automobile made by FORD.

Transportation

Lotus	British automobile; no longer manufactured.
Mack	The sturdy, chrome-plated bulldog that stands atop the hood of all Mack trucks.
Mazda	A Japanese automobile/manufacturer.
Mercedes	A German luxury automobile manufactured by Mercedes Benz.
MG	A British sports car.
Mitsubishi	A Japanese automobile/manufacturer.
Nissan	A Japanese automobile/manufacturer.
Peugeot	A French automobile/manufacturer.
Piper	An American aircraft.
Porsche	A German sports car.
Prelude	An automobile made by HONDA.
Rambler	An automobile manufactured in the United States; it is no longer in production.
Regal *yeah!*	An automobile made by BUICK.
Rolls Royce	A British luxury automobile/manufacturer.
Schooner	A sailing vessel with two or more masts.

Seville	A luxury automobile made by CADILLAC.
Steamer	An early, steam-powered automobile.
Sterling	A British automobile/manufacturer.
Subaru	A Japanese automobile/manufacturer.
Suzuki	A Japanese automobile/manufacturer.
T-Bird	Thunderbird: automobile made by FORD.
Toyota	A Japanese automobile/manufacturer.
Triumph	A British sports car.
Volkswagen	A German automobile/manufacturer.
Yamaha	A Japanese motorcycle/manufacturer.

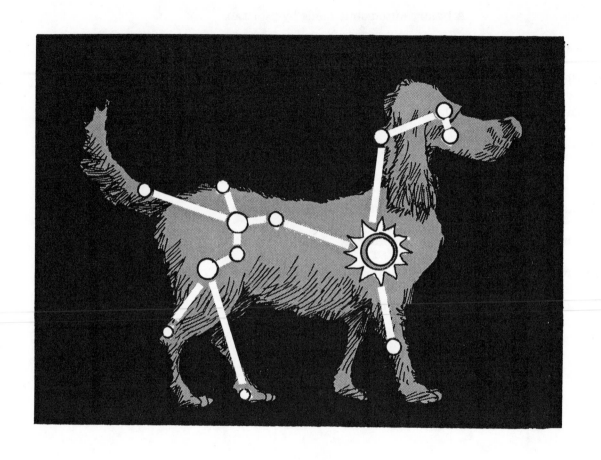

"Canis Major"

CHAPTER 18

Nature and Science

Nature gives to every time and season some beauties of its own; and from morning to night, as from cradle to the grave, is but a succession of changes so gentle and easy that we can scarcely mark their progress.

Charles Dickens

Take a look at the world of possibilities here. You very well may have a "Gamma" or a "Tiger Lily" just waiting to have the proper title bestowed upon him or her.

Acacia	Buckeye	Cosmos	Foxy
Acorn	Buckwheat	Cotton	Frog
Alfalfa	Buffalo	Crab	Fungus
Amino	Bull	Cub	Galaxy
Android	Bunny	Cyclone	Gamma
Anode	Buttercup	Daffodil	Garden
Argon	Butterfly	Daisy	'Gator
Ash	Byte	Dandelion	Goat
Ashes	Cactus	Dog	Goose
Aspen	Calf	Dove	Grizzly
Aster	Canis Major	Dynamite	Halo
Asteroid	Carnation	Eagle	Hawk
Astro	Cat	Earth	Hog
Aurora	Catfish	Eclipse	Holly
Axis	Cathode	Equinox	Honeysuckle
Azalea	Cheetah	Feather	Hormone
Badger	Chick	Felis	Horse
Bear	Cloud	Fern	Iguana
Beaver	Cobra	Fish	Iris
Bengal	Columbine	Fission	Ivy
Blossom	Comet	Flower	Jasmine
Bluebonnet	Coot	Fox	Jupiter
Boa	Coral	Foxfire	Kingfish
Bobcat	Corona	Foxtail	Krypton

Larkspur	Morning Glory	Primrose	Thunder
Laser	Mule	Rabbit	Tiger
Lava	Neon	Rainbow	Tiger Lily
Leech	Nova	Rose	Toad
Leopard	Nuke	Rosebud	Topaz
Lightning	Oleander	Sage	Tree
Lilac	Onyx	Sagebrush	Tulip
Lily	Orbit	Shark	Tumbleweed
Lizard	Orchid	Skunk	Turkey
Llama	Ozone	Snake	Turtle
Lotus	Panda	Snapdragon	Twilight
Lunar	Pansy	Solar	Venus
Magnolia	Panther	Spider	Weasel
Marigold	Parasite	Squirrel	Weed
Megabyte	Petunia	Star	Whale
Micro	Pig	Steroids	Willow
Micron	Pigeon	("Roids")	Wolf
Mink	Pluto	Sun	Worm
Mirage	Polar	Sunset	Zebra
Monkey	Poppy	Sunspot	Zinnia
Moon			

"Donut"

CHAPTER 19

Foods

. . . eat, that thou mayest have strength, when thou goest on thy way.

I *Samuel* 28:22

In every veterinarian's files, you will find many pets named after a variety of foods: from "Bagel" and "Biscuit" to "Taffy" and "Truffle." For a perfect pet praenomen, take a look at this sampling of culinary delights.

Foods

Angel Food

Apple

Asparagus

Baby Ruth (A brand of candy bar.)

Bagel

Banana

Basil

Beef

Berry

Biscuit

Blackberry

Blueberry

Bosco (A brand of chocolate syrup.)

Bromley (A type of apple.)

Brownie

Bubble Gum

Buttercup

Butterfingers (A brand of chocolate candy bar.)

Buttermilk

Caramel

Carrot

Cashew

Casserole

Caviar

Chalupa (A type of Mexican food consisting of a flat fried TORTILLA topped with refried beans and cheese.)

Cheddar

Cheerio (A brand of breakfast cereal.)

Cheesecake

Cheeto (A brand of cheese-flavored corn puff.)

Chestnut

Chicken

Chili

Chip(s)

Chiquita (A brand of bananas.)

Chocolate Chip

Chung King (A brand of Chinese food.)

Cinnamon

Cinnamon Muffin

Clove

Cocoa

Coconut

Coffee

Cookie ⚹

Crackers

Crepe (A thin pancake.)

Crisco (A brand of shortening.)

Crouton

Cupcake

Curry (A mixture of spices used in Indian cooking.)

Custard

Donut

Eggplant

Egg Roll

Enchilada (A type of Mexican food consisting of a TORTILLA filled with meat or cheese.)

Escargot (A French delicacy of snails prepared in butter, parsley, and garlic.)

Fajita (A type of Mexican food consisting of strips of barbequed meat, usually beef or chicken served with TORTILLAS.)

Frankfurter

French Fry

Frito (A brand of corn chip.)

Fudge

Ginger

Foods

Ginger Snap

Guacamole (Mashed and seasoned avacado.)

Gum Drop

Gummi Bear (A brand of candy.)

Häagen Dazs (A brand of ice cream.)

Hershey (A brand of chocolate.)

Honey

Hot Dog

Jello

Jelly

Jerky (A dried beef snack.)

Kibble (A type of dry dog food.)

Kiwi

Kumquat (A type of citrus fruit.)

Lemon Drop

Licorice

Linguini

Lollipop

Macaroni

Marshmallow

Meatball

Meringue (Stiffly beaten egg whites and sugar used as a dessert topping.)

Muffin

Mustard

Nacho (A type of Mexican food consisting of a chip topped with refried beans, cheese and/or jalapeño peppers.)

Noodle

Nutmeg

O. J. (Orange juice.)

Oatmeal

Olive

Onion

Oreo (A brand of cookie.)

Pancake

Paprika

Peaches

Peanut(s)

Pepper

Peppermint

Pepper Shaker

Phyllo (Paper-thin sheets of pastry used in the preparation of Greek desserts and appetizers.)

Pickles

Pistachio

Popcicle

Popcorn

Potato

Pretzel

Pumpkin

Quiche

Raisin

Raspberry

Relish

Ribeye

Ritz (A brand of cracker.)

Salt

Sassafras (A type of tea.)

Schnitzel

Sesame

Shortcake

Shrimp

Sirloin

Skippy (A brand of peanut butter.)

Foods

Snickers (A brand of candy bar.)

Soufflé

Soup

Spaghetti

Spearmint

Spice

Spud (Potato.)

Squash

Strawberry

Strudel

Sugar

Sushi (A type of Japanese food consisting of raw fish and seasoned rice.)

T-Bone

Tabasco (A brand of hot sauce.)

Taco (A type of Mexican food consisting of a folded TORTILLA filled with meat, cheese and spices.)

Taffy

Tamale (A type of Mexican food consisting of minced meat and spices rolled in a corn dough and cooked in a wrapping of a corn husk.)

Tater (Potato.)

Tenderloin

Tomato

Tootsie Roll

Tortilla (A type of Mexican food consisting of a thin baked circular piece of dough, the main ingredient being corn or flour.)

Truffle

Turnip

Twinkie (A brand of snack cake.)

Waffle

Wheatie(s) (A brand of breakfast cereal.)

Ziplock (A brand of food storage bags.)

"Brandy"

CHAPTER 20

Liquors and Drinks

Let your boat of life be light, packed with only what you need—a homely home and simple pleasures, one of two friends, worth the name, someone to love you, a cat, a dog, and a pipe or two, enough to eat and enough to drink; for thirst is a dangerous thing.

Jerome Klapka Jerome
from *Three Men in a Boat* (1889)

Belly up to the bar.

Undoubtedly some of the following names were selected after the pet owners did so. (Not all the drinks listed are alcoholic).

Cheers to you!

Liquors and Drinks

Amaretto	Almond LIQUEUR.
Bahama Mama	A cocktail.
Beaujolais	A type of red wine.
Beck's	A brand of German beer.
Big Red	A brand of soft drink.
Bourbon	A liquor distilled from a mash of corn, rye and malted barley.
Brandy	A liquor distilled from fermented grapes or other fruit.
Budweiser	A brand of American beer.
Candian Club (C. C.)	A brand of Canadian WHISKEY.
Cappucino	A drink made with strong coffee and hot milk.
Champagne	An effervescent wine.
Chivas (Regal)	A brand of Scotch WHISKEY
Claret	A type of red wine.
Coca-Cola (Coke)	A brand of soft drink.
Cocoa	A beverage made from the defatted portion of the cocoa bean.
Coffee	A beverage made from roasted and ground coffee beans.

Cognac	A type of French BRANDY.
Coors	An American beer
Corona	A brand of Mexican beer.
Courvoisier	A brand of French COGNAC.
Cuervo	A brand of Mexican TEQUILA.
Dewars	A brand of Scotch WHISKEY.
Dos Equis	A brand of Mexican beer.
Dr. Pepper	A brand of soft drink.
Gin	A liquor flavored with juniper berries.
Grolsch	A brand of Dutch beer.
Harvey Wallbanger	A cocktail.
Heineken	A brand of Dutch beer.
Hurricane	A cocktail.
Jack Daniels	A brand of Tennesee WHISKEY.
Jigger(s)	A measure used in making mixed drinks (usually 1½ ounces)
Kahlúa	A brand of Mexican coffee liqueur.

Liquors and Drinks

Kamikaze	A cocktail.
Lemonade	A beverage made with lemon juice, sugar, and water.
Liqueur	A sweetened, flavored liquor.
Mai Tai	A cocktail.
Margarita	A cocktail.
Martini	A cocktail.
Miller	A brand of American beer.
Mint Julep	A cocktail.
Mocha	A rich Arabian coffee; a drink made by mixing coffee with chocolate.
Moosehead	A brand of Canadian beer.
Mr. Pibb	A brand of soft drink.
Nehi	A brand of soft drink.
Old Milwaukee	A brand of American beer.
Pabst (Blue Ribbon)	A brand of American beer.
Pearl	A brand of Texas beer.
Pepe Lopez	A brand of Mexican TEQUILA.

Pepsi	A brand of soft drink.
R. C. Cola	A brand of soft drink.
Root Beer	A soft drink.
Sapporo	A brand of Japanese beer.
Schnapps	Various flavored LIQUEURS.
Scotch	A whiskey distilled from malted barley.
Seagram's	A brand of American blended WHISKEY.
Sebastiani	A California wine/winery.
Seven Up	A brand of soft drink.
Shasta	A brand of soft drink.
Singapore Sling	A cocktail.
Slice	A brand of soft drink.
Soda	A flavored soft drink; unflavored carbonated water; a mixture of the latter with ice cream and syrup.
Soda Pop	A flavored soft drink.
Sprite	A brand of soft drink.

Spritzer	A cocktail.
Stolychnaya (Stoli)	A brand of Russian VODKA.
St. Pauli Girl	A brand of German beer.
Stroh's	A brand of American beer.
Superior	A brand of Mexican beer.
Swizzle	A cocktail.
Tea	A beverage brewed from the leaves of the tea plant.
Tecate	A brand of Mexican beer.
Tequila	A liquor distilled from mescal.
Tonic	Anything that refreshes or rejuvenates; a regional carbonated water.
Two Fingers	A brand of Mexican TEQUILA.
Vodka	A colorless, "neutral" liquor distilled from grain.
Whiskey	Any liquor distilled from a grain mash.
Wild Turkey	A brand of Kentucky WHISKEY.
Xing Tao	A brand of Chinese beer.
Zinfandel	A red, white, or blush wine made from California's Zinfandel grape.

"Schnapps"

"L.L. Bean"

CHAPTER 21

Fashion and Cosmetics

The world is governed more by appearances than by realities, so that it is fully as necessary to seem to know something as to know it.

Daniel Webster

You don't have to be an ardent devotee of design to consider some of the names in this chapter. Just the right name for your fashionable pet might be close at hand . . . or on your feet!

Fashion and Cosmetics

Aca Joe	A brand of clothing.
Anaïs Anaïs	A brand of perfume.
Benetton	A brand of clothing.
Blush	A type of cosmetic used to heighten facial color.
Bongo	A brand of clothing.
Bubble Bath	A scented soap used to produce masses of bubbles in bath water.
Calvin Klein	Designer; brand of clothing.
Cambridge	A brand of clothing.
Cashmere	A fine woolen fabric made from the hair of the kashmir goat.
Chanel	Designer; brand of clothing and perfume.
Chic	A brand of clothing; highly fashionable.
Chloë	A brand of perfume.
Christian Dior	Designer; brand of clothing; perfume and cosmetics.
Claiborne (Liz)	Designer; brand of clothing and perfume.
Confetti	A brand of clothing.
Cover Girl	A brand of cosmetics.

Drakkar	A brand of cologne.
Elle	A fashion magazine.
Esprit	A brand of clothing.
Finesse	A brand of shampoo/hair products.
Forenza	A brand of clothing.
Genera	A brand of clothing.
Giorgio	A brand of perfume.
Girbaud	A brand of clothing.
Gitano	A brand of clothing.
Givenchy	Designer; brand of clothing, perfume, and cosmetics.
Gucci	Designer; brand of clothing, handbags, etc.
Guess	A brand of clothing.
Haggar	A brand of clothing.
Halston	Designer; brand of cologne and perfume.
Jasmine	A brand of perfume.
L. L. Bean	A mail-order clothing company and brand of outdoor clothing products.

Fashion and Cosmetics

Laura Ashley	Designer; brand of clothing, linens, and perfume.
Lee	A brand of sportswear.
Levi	A brand of sportswear.
Lipstick	A type of cosmetic used to heighten lip color.
Maybelline	A brand of cosmetics.
Obsession	A brand of perfume and cologne.
Opium	A brand of perfume and cologne.
Paisley	A multicolored pattern of curving shapes used to decorate fabric.
Paloma Picasso	Designer; daughter of artist Pablo Picasso.
Pappagallo	A brand of clothing.
Paris	A brand of perfume.
Pearl	A lustrous concretion formed inside an oyster.
Poison	A brand of perfume.
Polo	A brand of clothing designed by RALPH LAUREN.
Powder Puff	A fluffy applicator for face or body powder.
Ralph Lauren	Designer; brand of clothing.

Revlon	A brand of cosmetics.
Rolex	A brand of wristwatch.
Ruby	A precious stone.
Sapphire	A precious stone.
Satin	A lustrous fabric made of silk or rayon.
Shalimar	A brand of perfume.
Soapy	Sudsy.
Speigel	A mail-order clothing company.
Sterling	Silver that is nearly pure (925 parts silver to 75 parts copper).
Tiffany	A fashionable jewelry store in New York City.
Topaz	A semi-precious stone.
Tux	Short for tuxedo—formal attire for a man.
Vanderbilt (Gloria)	Designer; brand of clothing and perfume.
Vidal Sassoon	Designer; brand of clothing and hair-care products.
Wrangler	A brand of clothing.
Yves Saint Laurent	Designer; brand of clothing.

"Moritz" and *"Max"*

CHAPTER 22

Pairs

. . people . . . name (their) dogs
Pitter and Patter,
Willy and Nilly,
Helter and Skelter,
Namby and Pamby,
Hugger and Mugger, and even
Wishy and Washy,
Ups and Daisy,
Fitz and Startz,
Fetch and Carrie, and
Pro and Connie.

James Thurber
from "How to Name a Dog"

So you're having twice as much fun now that you have two little critters, right? You might as well relax and enjoy it by taking a look at these intersting combinations. Perhaps you'll find that very speical one-of-a-kind name for your very special two-of-a-kind friends.

Pairs

Adam & Eve (See Chapter 7)

Amos & Andy (See Chapter 11)

Antony & Cleopatra

Back & Forth

Baron & Baroness

Baucis & Philemon (See Chapter 6)

Bert & Ernie (See Chapter 11)

Biton & Cleobis (See Chapter 6)

Bogey & Bacall (See Chapter 11)

Bonnie & Clyde

Cagney & Lacey

Cain & Abel (See Chapter 7)

Calvin & Hobbes (See Chapter 14)

Castor & Pollux (See Chapter 6)

Count & Countess

Cupid & Psyche (See Chapter 6)

Czar & Czarina

David & Goliath (See Chapter 7)

Ding & Ling

Down & Out

Dr. Jekyll & Mr. Hyde

Dude & Dudette

Duke & Duchess

Emperor & Empress

Ferdinand & Isabella (See Chapter 5)

First & Ten

George & Gracie (See Chapter 11)

Hera & Zeus (See Chapter 6)

Hero & Leander (See Chapter 6)

Him & Her (See Chapter 5)

Hollywood & Vine

Itsy & Bitsy

Buddy & Winnie

King & Queen

Kut & Kutta (See Chapter 9)

Lady & Tramp (See Chapter 11)

Laurel & Hardy (See Chapter 11)

Lord & Lady

Love 'Em & Leave 'Em

Max & Moritz (See Chapter 10)

Mickey & Minnie (See Chapter 14)

Mutt & Jeff (See Chapter 14)

Napoleon & Josephine (See Chapter 5)

Now & Then

Orpheus & Eurydice (See Chapter 6)

Ozzie & Harriet (See Chapter 11)

Patience & Fortitude (See Chapter 10)

Patriarch & Matriarch

Prince & Princess

Pyramus & Thisbe (See Chapter 6)

Romeo & Juliet (See Chapter 10)

Ruff & Tuff

Salt & Pepper

Samson & Delila (See Chapter 7)

Scarlet & Rhett (See Chapter 11)

Simon & Garfunkel

Simon & Schuster (See Chapter 10)

Stanley & Livingstone (See Chapter 5)

Sugar & Spice

Tom & Jerry (See Chapter 14)

Topsy & Turvy

Waylon & Willy

When & If

Wilbur & Orville (See Chapter 5)

Registering a Name with the American Kennel Club

If your dog will be registered by the American Kennel Club (AKC), you need to follow the guidelines established by the AKC:

The person who owns the dog and applies to register it has the right to name the dog. On registration applications issued starting in mid-1989 a space is provided for only one name choice. Registration applications issued prior to that time have spaces for two name choices. It is not necessary to indicate a second name choice, but if you do, consider both names carefully. There is always a chance that the second will be approved and, therefore, it should be equally desirable by the owner. A dog's name may not be changed after it is registered.

Name choices are limited to 25 letters.

No Arabic or Roman numerals may be included in name choices, and no written number is permitted at the end of names. AKC reserves the right to assign a Roman numeral. AKC permits 37 dogs of each breed to be assigned the same name, and many common names such as Spot, Snoopy, Lassie, King, etc., are fully allotted. The shorter the name choice the greater the chances that AKC will assign a Roman numeral or that the name may not be accepted at all. The longer and more unique the name chosen, the greater the chance for approval. The easiest way to lengthen a name is to incorporate your surname, for example, "Smith's Spot" instead of "Spot."

Remember that the dog's "call name," that is, to the name he responds does not have to be the same as his registered name. If you name your dog "Spot" and it is not approved, you may continue to call him "Spot," even though his registered name may be different.

Incorrect spelling and grammar are not corrected by AKC. Names are approved as submitted. A change in spelling is considered a change of name and is not allowed.

Do not include:
1. Names of prominent people, living or recently deceased.
2. Words or abbreviations that imply AKC titles (Champ, Winner).
3. The words: Dog, Male, Sire, Bitch, Female, Dam, Kennel.
4. Words that are disparaging or obscene.
5. Roman or Arabic numerals.
6. Breed names alone.[*]

To obtain applications or more information concerning AKC registration and requirements, write to:

> American Kennel Club
> 51 Madison Avenue
> New York, New York 10010

[*]American Kennel Club, *Dogs, General Information,* (New York: American Kennel Club), pp. 21–22. Used with permission.

Help me make *The Best Pet Name Book Ever* even better!

Just in case I forgot your favorite pet name, please send it to me so I can include it in the next edition of this book.

If there is a story or explanation behind your choice of name, please include that, too.

Send all nominations for the next edition to:

Wayne Bryant Eldridge
c/o Barron's Educational Series, Inc.
250 Wireless Boulevard
Hauppauge, NY 11788